God's Astounding Opinion of You

RALPH HARRIS

HARVEST HOUSE PUBLISHERS

EUGENE, OREGON

GOD'S ASTOUNDING OPINION OF YOU
Copyright © 2007 by Ralph Harris
Published 2011 by Harvest House Publishers
Eugene, Oregon 97402
www.harvesthousepublishers.com

Library of Congress Cataloging-in-Publication Data
Harris, Ralph, 1956-
  [Better off than you think]
  God's astounding opinion of you / Ralph Harris.
    p. cm.
  Originally published: Better off than you think. Evangel Pub. House, ©2007
  ISBN 978-0-7369-3783-2 (pbk.)
  1. God (Christianity)—Love. 2. Christian life. 3. Spirituality. I. Title.
  BT140.H35 2011
  231'.6—dc22
                                                          2010021574

My deepest love and thanks to my delightful and blameless wife,
Sarah, and my dear and brilliant daughters, Ellen and Emma.
Without your encouragement, inspiration, and patience, my life
and this book would have all the seasoning of cottage cheese.

Contents

Foreword

Ralph Harris is an affirmer. I've noticed that in his interactions with other people. He almost always finds a way to let them know that they're valuable. Because he acts that way, he reminds me a lot of his heavenly Father. He sees the best in people and seems to call out those qualities within them to a greater degree by the words he says to and about them. I think it's Christ in Ralph who is doing that.

The book you hold in your hand is an expression of this gifting and ministry the Father has entrusted to Ralph. The first time I read this book, I felt a power in it. Not the heady kind of experience that can happen when somebody strokes your ego by flattery, but a sense of empowerment. Ralph was telling me authentic truths about my identity that I already knew deep within myself, but I found benefit in having them reinforced.

God's Astounding Opinion of You isn't one of those books that's supposed to get you hyped up over believing in yourself. To the contrary, this book will cause you to become genuinely enthused about the One who created you. It will cause you to sense love for Him rising up in you in response to the lavishing love He has for you. You're going to feel that love as you read this book. You're going to believe what Ralph tells you about your Father's opinion because he backs it up with Scripture and the Holy Spirit is going to assure you that it's true.

I believe anybody who reads this book will be a better person for having read it. It's not simply a better self-image that we all need, but a *biblical* self-image. That's the value of this book. It sets forth biblical truth about who you are as the beloved child of God and motivates you to believe it despite messages to the contrary that you may have received during your lifetime.

When you discover the reality of *God's Astounding Opinion of You*, you're going to find yourself being transformed. Love is the greatest power for transformation that exists, and the greatest love that exists is the *agape* of God. As simple as it seems, our determined attempts to improve ourselves or even our sincere prayers for God to help us change do not facilitate transformation. What revolutionizes lives is the love of the Father at work in us through His Son and by the power of His Spirit. That's what will happen to you as you read.

Some books are enjoyable but forgettable. Others are memorable and inspirational. Now and then you'll come across one that is transformational. This book fits in the last category. Open your heart and mind as you read it. Ask the Holy Spirit to take away any barriers that could prevent you from believing that you are as wonderfully lovable as this book will suggest you are. Then read it with a hungry heart and I guarantee you won't be disappointed.

Steve McVey
Author, *Grace Walk*

Introduction

Come to me, all you who are weary and burdened, and I
will give you rest. Take my yoke upon you and learn from me,
for I am gentle and humble in heart, and you will find rest
for your souls. For my yoke is easy and my burden is light.

MATTHEW 11:28-30

You're in for the greatest of delights if you are familiar with the
above passage but not so familiar with the experience.

The single purpose of this book is that you find Jesus and life in
Christ—Christianity—deeply satisfying, beyond anything you've
ever known. Many of us, long haunted by the above passage, know
Jesus said it, but our desire to know it in experience has been relatively frustrated.

I believe the current work of God is centered upon the theme
found above, with the immediate benefit being a happy bunch of
God-enamored Christians—it's what God is doing today. While
works *for* God are important, the work *of* God in His people should
thrill us so much that we become crazy about and gladly dependent
on Him. And that's what life is like when you find Him in you as
well as around you. The great joy you find will certainly produce
sincere works for God, but that's not God's first goal—it's the result.
Works for God are a by-product of grace-filled believers who cannot
contain the wonderful, deep urgings and desires of the Spirit living
within. This is the inheritance of those purchased by Jesus Christ,
and He is determined you should have it.

It begins with knowing what God thinks of you. At a seemingly record pace, God is making new and fantastic sons and daughters, tremendous children of His glory through the new birth in Christ. How thrilling is the church—and how thrilling are you! One moment we're in serious trouble with God, and the next we're spot-on perfect, indwelt by God Himself, residents of heaven already, the people of God's delight. What a change! Yet most days, that change makes little difference to us. We've lost (or have never known) the wonder of the miracle that began with Jesus, "the firstborn among many brothers" (Romans 8:29).

Why? Because we've been deluded into making a lunatic argument with God. The argument is not so much about who He is and what He is capable of doing. It's about who we are and our role in His plan. While He thinks we're one thing—holy, righteous, blameless, and majestic sons and daughters walking the planet—we think we're something else…something way less. God's opinion of us and our opinion of ourselves don't agree. Based on what He did for us through the death and resurrection of Christ centuries ago, He has been making fabulous new creations, actual brothers and sisters of Jesus, for centuries since. But what do we think? *If I'm a brother of Jesus, as bad as I am, I must be the black sheep of God's family!* And only Satan, the chief lunatic, enjoys the joke.

With that disagreement as our starting point, it's not hard to imagine why our experience with God falls sadly short of our inheritance. Fortunately, God is fed-up with it! He is happily working to awaken us to what He knows is true concerning us so we may live as we are in Christ—the *astounding* children of God!

So prepare yourself—God is working to impress and convince you of what He has done for you and in you. It's a labor He really enjoys! As He increasingly wins you over to His way of thinking about you, you'll increasingly live *as* you really are because you'll know *who* you really are. When your opinion of yourself matches up with God's opinion of you, and when who you are lines up with how you live, the glory of God will be stunningly evident! And you'll be living by faith.

You're going to love what you find through the pages of this book. In fact, you can even take notes on what you learned in the "Personal Notes" section at the end.) Its message will transform you and become the most natural and satisfying way for you to live. You've been made for that kind of life, and it's time you had it.

Chapter One

Salieri's Game

The Enemy's Strategy to Keep You from You

So we fix our eyes not on what is seen, but on what is unseen.
For what is seen is temporary, but what is unseen is eternal.

2 CORINTHIANS 4:18

All deception in the course of life is indeed nothing else but a lie
reduced to practice, and falsehood passing from words into things.

ROBERT SOUTHEY

Not long ago my wife and I had a home built for us here in Colorado. Having departed the stuffy congestion of Southern California, the expanse of the Rocky Mountains was wonderfully invigorating. Everything seemed new, which—in our case, at least—begged for new plans. Nearly everyone enjoyed our enthusiasm and did what they could to assist the rookies in the Rockies. Our home builders worked diligently, landscaping our front yard with Colorado staples such as river rock, aspens, and meadowlike shrubbery. It seemed like the team of workers had it all done perfectly in 15 minutes. Unfortunately, the backyard was not part of the deal—they left that for me.

Looking at my lineage, anyone would know why I was ill-equipped to tackle such a task. Generations of males in my family have been virtually clueless around lumber, pipe, and cement. Spend five seconds in my garage, and you'll know I'm not one of those guys who has every tool known to mankind perfectly laid out or hung up and who is anxiously anticipating a mission to Home

Depot over the weekend. The only reason I have any tools at all is because I had to buy them to use immediately—like a hammer.

But because we didn't want our daughters playing in a dirt backyard for the next five years, we carefully constructed a meticulous plan. After months of regular wrestling with dirt, trees, rock, shrubs, and demonic sprinkler lines, I felt I had broken out of the cursed line of ineptitude. A perceptive few confirmed my breakout by saying, "Wow. We didn't think you had it in you. *It actually looks good.*"

Finally, the day came for the crowning deed—the laying of the sod. After we had it in place, we christened it with delicately sprinkled water from our perfectly placed sprinklers and celebrated the flawless completion of our plan. Luxurious and unblemished, the forest green lawn proclaimed our magnificent success.

But there was a problem. Out of our eyesight, our lawn was playing the harlot. In what seemed like no time at all, we became convinced that our pristine fescue had been beckoning every nasty plant seed in our state to lay with it. Ugly offspring soon popped out all over our backyard, revealing what had been happening in the darkness without our knowledge and without our permission. Having planned so carefully and worked so hard, I thought my labor was virtually over—I could just stand back and enjoy the view. But for months on end, what greeted a look out any rear window were weeds, weeds, and more weeds.

We hadn't recognized the terrible effect something unseen and unknown could have on our plans. From those days to these, it's war in our backyard. Only now we know what's going on out of sight, and we're fighting a little smarter.

The Unseen Arena

The most important arena is not the one right in front of us, the one we can see, but the one out of sight, the one we cannot see. The real story is not first visible but invisible. Long ago God planned for His story, beginning to end, to unfold visibly over centuries of time. Since you and I first began our life of faith, we've been reading our

Bibles and looking to that invisible story more and more—it has our attention. Even if we don't look any different and even if the world around us doesn't look any different, our understanding of it all is *far different.*

We now know that there's a lot going on unseen, and it fashions our faith and shapes what we experience. We're learning that, in order to live in the visible, we must put our faith in the invisible. This is how we get to know God, and it's also how we get to know ourselves. From the moment the Garden doors were shut to Adam and Eve, man's greatest effort has been to live by faith in what he cannot see.

Our faith will drift rudderless if we don't know what's true and happening in the invisible arena. We'll be left confused and frustrated in the visible because that's where God's story is playing out, and we'll be left to pulling mysterious weeds out of our lives all of our days. But if we discover and believe what God says is true and important in the unseen, life will begin to make sense and excel— we will have the life that was promised by our Lord Jesus.

What God Thinks of You

In this book we'll look at what God thinks of Himself, but we'll concern ourselves primarily with what God thinks of you. Why is that important? If God and you disagree about who and what you are, your approach to Him and your approach to all of life will be a tangled mess. It cannot be otherwise.

This isn't a book on self-esteem with the goal that, after reading it, you'll feel better about yourself. That's not nearly enough. It is a book about accurate self-estimation based entirely upon what God thinks of you, and without question, you'll feel way better about yourself at the end. For the Christian, self-esteem isn't something you work up and get so you can live well. It's something you receive from God because you *are* well—now go and live! He loves it and is glorified when we believe Him about ourselves and live accordingly. That's the goal.

Fortunately, the way to it will be surprising and incredibly invigorating because it's certain that God thinks you're better than you do and that you're better off in life than you think. (By the way, He's right!)

God thinks He has made you a fantastic, Spirit-born person, quite a bit like Himself, well-recognized throughout the heavens. If you could right now take a poll of those in the heavenlies, they would all tell you how much you resemble Him. Of course, you'd have to be wary of those of the Liar Clan; they, after all, would lie. But even those on the demonic side of things know the truth about you. You should too.

You're different. And while you have a residence, an identity (mom, dad, brother, sister, lawyer, salesman...), responsibilities, and more, those earthly things are, at best, nice accessories for you and cannot ever match up to the truth about you. No matter how great and excellent your title, no matter how good your family, no matter how great your lawn looks, any identity you may have in the visible realm will never be as good as the identity you have in the invisible realm. It's what makes you different.

For sure, it's better than you think and *it's more real than anything else.* More than likely, you'll have to be weaned from focusing upon the various titles and roles this visible world has to offer in order to see the majesty of the invisible and to have it count for something. It might not be easy.

You Are Not of This World

Let me show you what I mean. If I told you that Jesus compared believers to Himself, how would you think we might stack up? It's better than you might believe, and it's fundamentally critical you believe it. Speaking about the people the Father had given to Him, Jesus said, "My prayer is not that you take them out of the world but that you protect them from the evil one. They are not of the world, *even as* I am not of it" (John 17:15-16).

According to God, we're not of this world to the same extent He is not—we match with Him! Can you believe it? You are not *from* or *of* this world any longer, your natural birth having been overcome by your supernatural birth. One began your life, while the other changed it. One birth was of this world, while the other was of another—you're from the same place God is! That's what He thinks; how about you?

Through your new birth in Christ, God changed you from having the same earth-born nature as those still of this world, and now you're actually *of* Him, sharing in His very nature. You're now far more like Him at the center of your being than you will ever again be like the people of this world. You *are* different, and He wants everyone and everything to know about the great work He has done with you. He brags on you, and you might as well know why.

Not aware of how like Him you have become? It's probably because you've accepted and grown accustomed to what this visible world says about you: who you are, what you are, and how you are. Someone invisible labors night and day so that you will have this mistaken identity.

Satan works to fool believers into believing they are better related to the world they can see than they are to the world they cannot see. In essence, *Satan doesn't want you to believe what God thinks of Himself and what God thinks about you.* He's been at work concerning what Christians believe about themselves for a long, long time, employing brilliant tactics against them.

Salieri

This scheme is well-portrayed in the terrific 1984 Academy Award-winning film *Amadeus*. Best Actor winner F. Murray Abraham plays Antonio Salieri, the court-appointed composer to the king of Austria. A talented composer in his own right, Salieri discovers and quickly begins to resent a rather gifted, spotlight-worthy composer, Wolfgang Amadeus Mozart.

Soon Salieri figures out that God lives in Mozart. That He does is made especially obvious by the fact that while Salieri works endless hours and even years to compose anything of any merit, Mozart dashes off the greatest musical pieces ever known virtually overnight and with ease: "As if he were taking dictation!" Salieri hisses. And it galls him, making him furious with God.

Sitting alone and brooding before a large and impressive crucifix, Salieri pulls down the emblem and sets it into a blazing fire, saying to Jesus concerning Mozart, "From now on, we are enemies, You and I. I will block You. I swear it! I will hinder and harm Your creature on earth as far as I am able. I will ruin Your incarnation!" For the remainder of the film, Salieri lives to frustrate the God-indwelt Mozart, robbing him of any recognition or joy of the gift of God within him. He is brutally successful, and finally, Mozart wears out and dies a poor man—alone, unhappy, and unfulfilled. Generations since have marveled at the obvious gift of God in Mozart, celebrating God in their love for his music, but Mozart had that joy and knowledge stolen from him. We know who was in Mozart, but Salieri's game was to make certain Mozart did not.

It was Satan's game then, and it remains his game today—don't let people know where the invisible God is. Let them think He is *out there*, but don't let them believe He is *in here*. It's a pretty good game, don't you think?

How long has it been since you've marveled at the fact of "Jesus in me!" or had a genuine bit of delight over Him living in you or a good leap for the joy of it? Has it been a while? Then I think the game is against you. I think "Salieri" has been about his business with you, seducing you into siding with his estimation of you ("You're nothing special—*just look at you*") and perhaps of others as well.

That's the game, and if he can, he'll get you to play along. Don't think about whether or not the invisible God lives in people and approach them accordingly. Think of them according to what they do and how they're doing at life. Think of people based upon what you can see, not based upon what you cannot see. After all, who can say what people are really like when you can't see them, right?

Wrong! If God is in the vessel, then you do know what they're really like. They're sons or daughters of God, and they are not best seen by what is visible but by what is invisible!

Remember the World You're From

Do you see?

If we don't see this, we'll be overwhelmed by the visible, and our approach to all of life will be twisted. It cannot be any other way. Dominated by the visible, our attraction to it will become a form of addiction—we'll value and live for it more than we'll value and live for the invisible. The affects will be disastrous because we'll be living not *as we are*, but *as we think we are*. The truth won't have us—a lie will. And nobody lives well in a lie.

Satan would have you to estimate yourself based not upon the world you're *from*, but upon the world you're *in*. And that will not do.

Paul emphasized this truth to the believers in Colossae:

> I have become its [the church's] servant by the commission God gave me to present to you the word of God in its fullness—the mystery that has been kept hidden for ages and generations, but is now disclosed to the saints. To them God has chosen to make known among the Gentiles the glorious riches of this mystery, which is *Christ in you*, the hope of glory. We proclaim him, admonishing and teaching everyone with all wisdom, so that we may present everyone perfect in Christ. To this end I labor, struggling with all his energy, which so powerfully works in me (Colossians 1:25-29).

It would be the pinnacle of understatement to say that for centuries, being "near to God" was not without serious issues. Following Him meant incredible, tragic, strange, and wondrous things would happen. But God *in* man! Is He serious? Think of it—God's likes and dislikes, God's loves, God's abilities, and God Himself within man. Consider how He would stand out from there! It would be obvious.

And that's the plan. Perfect. But it's not easy to walk around in your day thinking, *God is in me right now, at this very moment and will not leave me.* There may not be much to support that visibly. Nevertheless, facts are facts.

Things Are Different Now

But it wasn't always this way. During God's relationship with man under the old covenant, was anyone ever told to offer himself to God? No. Not once. Why not? No one was ever good enough, no one was ever entirely without blame or sin, and so the intimate presence of God was denied him. A spotless, unblemished, and entirely perfect animal was to be offered in his place. That was acceptable.

Is it the same now with the new covenant? Not at all! "Therefore, I urge you, brothers, in view of God's mercy, to *offer your bodies* as living sacrifices, holy and pleasing to God—this is your spiritual act of worship" (Romans 12:1).

Offering your body is an act of worship because you believe what He says about you, the offering: You've been made "holy and pleasing to God"! Through Christ, you've become perfectly acceptable. He didn't make you just a believer; He made you an excellent place in which to live. You're compatible! You probably don't always feel as if He's at home in you or He's entirely happy about His new digs. Yet faith looks to the invisible—not to the touchy-feely—and you know He's there because He says so.

Further, during the former covenant, would anyone have gotten together with a few friends, enjoyed some nice Egyptian ale, and at around midnight sneaked into the Holy of Holies? *No, sir!* Why not? *Because God was in there!* Nobody entered that holy place unless he was the high priest—and then only once a year. It's not at all difficult to imagine he had been prayed-up for weeks and took plenty of the blood of a spotless lamb with him. You didn't mess with the Holy of Holies because God *Himself* was in that temple.

Has it ever struck you that today God's Holy of Holies, the temple where God lives, is *reading this right now?*

Think for a moment on Paul's words to those sloppy Corinthian Christians: "Don't you know that you yourselves are God's temple and that God's Spirit lives in you? If anyone destroys God's temple, God will destroy him; *for God's temple is sacred, and you are that temple*" (1 Corinthians 3:16-17).

Have you thought of it? After finishing your morning coffee and walking out the door to work, have you thought, "Well, here I go, God's sacred mobile home into the day"? No? You're not dumb—Satan's been at work addicting you to the visible so that you find it difficult to live in the invisible. And faith is frustrated.

Peter and the Gentiles

He worked on Peter too. Because he had been absent from the God-is-making-all-things-new class, Peter received from the Spirit a nightmare revelation that his assessment of people was a tad bit off. Three times Peter was given a dream filled with nasty-looking, non-kosher creatures, which he assumed were in nature as they looked—*nasty.* Not so.

Correcting Peter's view of people and of Gentiles in particular, the Spirit said to him, "Do not call anything impure that God has made clean" (Acts 10:15). In other words, if God has made something brand-new or if God has come to live in a man (1 John 4:13), then regardless of his look, attitude, or behavior, he is *brand-new,* and God has made for Himself a holy, earthly dwelling place.

Satan knew this, and he fought against it. He fights still. Tactics? Focus the ones forever changed on the forever changing; swap the invisible for the visible. That'll do it.

Knowing the tactic, Paul cautions and instructs believers where to look in order to live. "So we fix our eyes not on what is seen, but on what is unseen. For what is seen is temporary, but what is unseen is eternal" (2 Corinthians 4:18).

If according to God we've become brand-new creations, entirely new creatures (2 Corinthians 5:17) and no longer of this world, then where is that visible? In the invisible! It's in the unseen eternal, in the never-changing arena that we are known for who we really are! Having been changed into sons and daughters of God, a look to the unseen arena will always reveal the truth of who we have become. That's why Paul urges us to keep our gaze *there*, fixing our hearts and thoughts *there*. In the unseen is where we'll find who we really are at all times, during any experience or condition in the visible temporary that is passing away. We don't "set our hearts on things above" (Colossians 3:1) in order to feel better about things below. We do it because that's where we'll find ourselves! We're known *there* but we're fairly unrecognizable *here*. *There* (in the unseen, perfectly real, eternal realm), we're got-it-goin'-on, stand-up-and-shout sons and daughters of God. *Here* (in the visible, temporary realm), we don't always look so good.

Don't Be Transfixed by the Visible

Where do you suppose Satan would like to galvanize our gaze, *there* or *here*? If he can attract the not-of-this-world sons and daughters of God to the things and situations of this passing-away stage, *here*, might he then be able to affect their thinking? Might he be able to pull off the scam of the millennium by seducing them into believing they are what they do and feel (and they are how they behave and think *here*) more so than what God says they truly are *there*? Do you suppose the devil could disrupt their faith—their belief about God and about themselves in relation to Him—and point it away from their native land (the heavenly realm) by bending it to earthly things? With a nod to Groucho Marx, you bet your life.

And it's not hard to hear again Salieri's words to Jesus about the talented Mozart: "I will block You, I swear it! I will hinder and harm Your creature on earth as far as I am able. I will ruin Your incarnation!"

So here's what's happened: By demonic concoction, many of us have come to believe that our behavior and thought life reveals more about who and what we are than what the Bible says about who and what we are. Perhaps we're straight theologically (it's tucked away somewhere in our heads), but practically and dominantly, we're twisted and have the two realms—invisible and visible—entangled. When that happens, we exchange the unseen (always true and unchanging) for the seen (temporary and changing) *as reality,* and then everything gets distorted—including our lives.

We've affixed our gaze on the wrong place. Scripture tells us the importance of shifting our assessment of people away from how they look or behave to whether they have had a second birth. Although we are to no longer regard anyone from a worldly point of view (2 Corinthians 5:16), we still fall prey to the temporary temptation. When we see our failures, struggles, and shortcomings, we begin to believe we are truly a mess in need of a lot of changes. What's wrong with that? Soon we'll become fascinated and fixated with ourselves instead of God. And that's tragic.

Transfixed by the visible, the practical relevance of the invisible will slip away, and eternal truth will begin to miss the mark of the heart. We'll begin to implore God to work on us, our misplaced faith missing the fact that He already has. And the separating identification of *there* and *here,* of eternal and temporal, is lost. The practicalities of faith are muddled and confused. What Jesus achieved for Himself by the cross and resurrection, the joy of making many the very sons and daughters of God, is frustrated. *That was Salieri's game.* And that's the tactic the devil has been using for a long time.

Brennan Manning writes the following:

> The paltriness of our lives is largely due to our fascination with the trinkets and trophies of the unreal world that is passing away…When we are not profoundly affected by the treasure in our grasp, apathy and mediocrity are inevitable. If passion is not to degenerate into nostalgia or sentimentality, it must renew itself at its source. The treasure is Jesus Christ. He is the Kingdom within.*

---

* Brennan Manning, *Abba's Child* (Colorado Springs, CO: NavPress, 2002), 8.

What to do? Where to start? Ask the Holy Spirit to expose every lie you might unwittingly believe, any subtle deception concerning what God thinks of you, what you are, and who you are with Him and how that affects your life. He will do it, and you'll find it to be one of the most exhilarating exercises you'll ever undertake. It's also the beginning of a whole new kind of love affair, one which changes your life by bringing you out.

And you'll love that.

Questions for Discussion

1. In this chapter, we have discussed how different (better!) your identity is in the invisible realm. What do you think about that?

2. If "looking at the invisible" seemed impractical to you, please explain why.

3. How effective has "Salieri" been at hiding you from you?

4. What are some of your hopes for the rest of the book?

Chapter Two

The Pursuit of Trivial Nobility

Jumping the Treadmill of Dissatisfying Delusion

The creation waits in eager expectation for
the sons of God to be revealed.

ROMANS 8:19

In Gaul were two orders, the nobility and the priesthood,
while the people, says Caesar, were all slaves.

JOHN LOTHROP MOTLEY

S o how does Satan do it? If what's true about God and us is fantastic beyond measure, and if all creation longs for the sons and daughters of God to be revealed as they are, majesty unveiled, how does the devil keep us from taking a look? He makes it relatively irrelevant. And he starts early.

Growing up in Southern California during the '60s and '70s, I found that perhaps my greatest challenge was to learn the skills necessary to win over the people I thought worthy of my efforts. The sports fields, hallways, and classrooms of my young life were dignified by a desirable class of nobility whose faces and physiques resembled the gods of Greek mythology (or of Hollywood), whose athletic prowess rivaled legend, and whose scholastic achievement assured them the best places in life. Some of us noticed the nobility, and we longed for it. For those of us who did, a sort of clandestine covetousness crept into our hearts, urging us to join the royals through well-employed techniques sure to gain their acceptance.

Some of us used humor and wit in the hope of joining the elite, and as we grew up, some of us sought to impress through the arts, while still others offered to secure alcohol or even drugs for the gods. Whatever the attempt, admission to nobility was the goal. I suspect ancient Rome must have looked somewhat the same.

Although the nobles generally remained noble, and few entered their ranks without the goods for genuine acceptance and deserved pomp, many of us wannabe nobles learned something ruinous: *We learned how to live as pretenders.* Rejection did not mean an end to our pursuit because the desire still plagued us! Although we believed the nobility before us was true nobility, few of us made the effort to resign ourselves to contented serfdom and a life lived in service to nobility. Instead, a twisted way of life formed that offered some small hope of successful arrival at the town of Aristocracy. Worse yet, a deception took root revealed by the effort: *We believed we were unfit.* We could do no better than act upon that lie.

"Do You Know Jesus?"

Following high school, the college campus provided the perfect opportunity for me to start all over again. Embracing the pretender way of life, I *arrived* as a nobleman, no one the wiser. There I could offer my practiced persona and make my way further up the ladder. What a stage it was—and with a much larger audience.

My little world of desire and experience, it seems, was not so unique. Little did I know that most everyone was making the same attempt as mine, scanning the fields of people, harvesting the look and behavior that achieved a notch up the hierarchy, and offering it as their own. Everyone was everyone's audience. Selection to an honor society, acceptance into a high-standing fraternal organization, a good-looking girlfriend on the arm, an excellent internship, or the reward of a desirable position of employment were the marks of burgeoning nobility and the validation of our pursuit amongst the masses.

We all knew the look, and we all watched each other's attempts at recognizable superiority, fearing the dreaded label and lot of the mediocre. My work paid off, and I made the grade, gaining membership in the necessary organizations and completing the picture with the just-right girlfriend. I looked noble!

Strutting around campus one day, I was approached by a seemingly safe, middle-aged woman who, blocking my way, asked, "Do you know Jesus? Do you *know* Him?"

Strangely enough, I had never before been asked that question, though I had grown up attending church fairly regularly. My answer was a sloppy, undignified, "Ugh, um, well, no, not like that. I mean, do I *know* Him? No. Not like that."

Looking into my eyes she asked, "Do you want to?"

I responded, "Well, no, not right now." After all, I was gloriously busy, and I was finally having a life I wanted.

She left me with a stab to my heart: "One day I think you will. You're not like all of this, and I think one day you will."

I never saw her again. I never forgot her either.

At that time, I was certain of only a couple of things, one of which was that Jesus was a cosmic killjoy. You didn't want to get mixed up with Him because your fun factor was sure to drop off—as in falling off a cliff. That lady bothered me, so I was glad to be rid of her so that I could get back to my increasingly successful life.

Not like all of this? I thought. *Oh, yes I am. I'm the best of it too. Move aside, lady. I'm on my way.*

Up the Ladder of Success

Several years later, with tons of education under my hat and the seeming respect of my peers, I launched my career. I had the tools. I had the skills. I had the pedigree and the skins on the wall. And to top it all off? *I finally got God.* That's right, I had finally accepted Him into my life. It happened after I was told that He would not only forgive me of my sins but also make my life even better than it already was. Wow! *Super*nobility!

Frankly, I hadn't been sure about *eternity*, an intimidating word meaning forever and ever and ever. I believed in Jesus and did some of the things I thought He wanted, and I didn't do some of the things I thought He didn't want me to do, but still…I had fairly well earned my nobility among my peers, carefully maintaining it and keeping it close. But what of *His* approval? And the question bouncing around the inside of my head where no one knew about it was, "What do I have to do to impress Him enough?" And the haunting fear, one from my earlier days of pretending, found a new arena— a new nobility to impress and join—if only I could.

I accepted the challenge, "accepted" His invitation to become a Christian and shortly set about to add this new recognizable royalty to my repertoire. In short order, I was carrying the "right" Bible, had a fish sticker on my car, had a proper pendant around my neck, and had begun teaching Bible studies and children's Sunday school.

Now I had everything! I was set. I was sure to succeed and sure to impress, and no matter the arena, I was complete. Business skills? I had my degree. Social acumen? Long practiced, a veteran. Athletic? In just about every sport I could compete—bring it on. And spirituality? Now I was even attractive there. I could do it all. Just let me prove it. (I spent years in the attempt.)

Here's what happened. I began to experience that high gift of good Christian living—*stress*. In my day-to-day life, it seemed to me that I now held dual citizenship—earthly and heavenly—with standards and requirements for both. On the one hand, earthly nobility had lots of requirements, most of which were coming along quite nicely, thank you very much. As a salesman, there were clients to impress and contracts to secure, competitors to subdue and bosses to schmooze. On the other hand, my Christian link meant there was God to impress, fellow Christians to inspire, a kingdom to advance, and enemies to thwart.

So several times a week, I sowed seeds in invisible, spiritual fields, and the rest of the time, I learned how to employ "kingdom principles" to advance my visible kingdom all the more. Maybe you know the effort: If I tithe, lucrative contracts will flow like milk and honey. If I pray for my boss, favor will rain from above. If I'm honest and

humble, I'll be a man of integrity, certain to be exalted. If I watch my
mouth and bless others, I will be blessed. And I should work hard—
drat, but okay. I can do that.

Backing into Prayer

But when I noticed that I was consistently measuring my *invisible* life and stature (that which I had with God) by my *visible* life
and stature, I began to feel uneasy. If I didn't get a particular contract, if a boss didn't notice me in the way I hoped, or if a longed-
for relationship with the woman of my dreams failed to materialize,
I believed something was wrong with me. Sure, I could chalk it up
to God and His sovereignty, but what if I was missing something or
doing something wrong, which, if fixed, might make things better?
Shouldn't I figure it out? Didn't God want me to figure it out? So I
set about to discover what was keeping me unfit and undeserving—
reading books, attending seminars, and praying harder for things to
be better. Weren't they supposed to be? Wouldn't they be if I prayed
just right and for a long enough time?

Do you ever back into prayer? You know, enter His throne room
by apologizing for nearly everything under the sun because you
know you're guilty of plenty, and the only way out is by lengthy
repentance? (You'd confess global warming if it would help.) I was
trying it out as my new angle with God, when one night, during
the lamentations part of my prayer, I heard the Spirit say something
odd, in direct conflict with my self-deprecating prayer time. As I
expressed regret about who knows what, I said something like, "You
know how I am, Lord." And before I could go on with my theme,
into my mind crashed the following:

*I do, but you do not. I find not one fault with you and love you endlessly. I have made you just right—perfect—and I love you. It is well
between you and Me.*

Pardon me? I thought. *Are You talking to* me? What did He know
that I did not? You know the word *flabbergasted?* I was that. But as it
is with God, His words to me came with life and strength, making

them gloriously undeniable. He sounded convinced—who was I to argue? Like a teenager who had just read a love letter from the most desirable girl in school, I reveled in His opinion of me and was instantly obsessed with Him. I did nearly everything I could to find out what He thought of me. After all, if He thought it, and if it turned out to be good—even great—then not only was I altogether different than I had supposed, but so was my life. No pretending necessary. And, unlike the charmed school girl, He never wavered in His amazing opinion of me.

So I devoured the New Testament. I discovered that I had been in a serious disagreement with God, believing I was something very different from what He knew I was. He thought I was something fantastic, and I thought I was something lowly—how could that not cause stress? I disagreed with Him! What I believed about who I was as a Christian was little different from what I believed about who I was in the world. Born something of a misfit, I had to work hard to reverse the assessment and change myself into something royal in both places. What a lot of work!

Because I believed it, I was valiantly attempting to be just right in both places and to live contentedly with dual citizenship. And that is simply not possible; one is far better than the other, and it must win out. The prized nobility of this world, which I had been rigorously pursuing, was exposed as comparatively inconsequential, filthy rags. What I was in His opinion was far better than anything I could ever have become or achieved in this world. The true nobility given me through the new birth in Christ made every other pursuit of worldly nobility trivial in comparison, even contradictory. It's that good, it's that high, it's that real.

I believe the confused ranks of today's wannabe nobles are legion, and they're filing past each other day after day, attempting the climb up the visible ladder of success. They reside in offices and stadiums, restaurants and schools, and—far worse—churches. Having grown up with the illusion that there was nothing better than the visual nobility offered through a chosen educational and career path, what appeals most is practical, how-to-make-it-happen sermons, books, and seminars, many of which encourage the illusory pursuit. The offer of a visibly better life is a powerful lure, and it often wins out over the discovery of who God has made us in Christ and how then to live. To be sure, we must pursue something, but if our adversary can keep us relatively disinterested in who and what we have become through the new birth, our pursuit of life will keep us making mud bricks in Egypt! There will be no joy in it because we're not fit for it. The other pursuit, the path which marvels at God's grand opinion of us, means genuine awe and delight, revelation from the Spirit, promised new life, and a timely death to a contradictory way of living.

If you were the devil, for which one would you vote?

Perfect People

The way forward is to first recognize *something incredible has happened*, which in turn has caused *something incredible to happen to you*. You didn't deserve it, and you may not know it, but a profound change has taken place. Referring to Jesus, the author of the book of Hebrews spells it out for us:

> Then he said, "Here I am, I have come to do your will."
> He sets aside the first [covenant] to establish the second.
> And by that will, *we have been made holy* through the sacrifice of the body of Jesus Christ once for all. Day after day every priest stands and performs his religious duties; again and again he offers the same sacrifices, which can never take away sins. But when this priest had offered for all time one sacrifice for sins, he sat down at the right hand of God. Since that time he waits for his enemies to be made his footstool, because *by one sacrifice he has made perfect forever those who are being made holy* (Hebrews 10:9-14).

Think of that. The Bible says that God, through the sacrifice of Jesus Christ, has made us holy already and that He has already

perfected those of us who are in Christ. Doesn't that seem preposterous? Scripture says that in Christ, we've already become the righteousness of God (see 2 Corinthians 5:21) and that we've been made
flawless and beyond accusation (see Colossians 1:22), sharing in His
nature (see 2 Peter 1:4). It seems ridiculous! But it's true. Where? As
we saw in chapter 1, it's true *there*, in the invisible, eternal realm! And
for how long will it be true? For how long will we be the holy, perfect, flawless, and beyond-accusation sons and daughters of God?
For always! The Bible uses all kinds of marvelous words and phrases
to describe us as we have already become in Christ, forever estab-
lishing how great His gift is to us. It is perhaps the most humbling
point of faith to believe what He believes is true about you, and the
wonder of it makes you addicted to the One holding the opinion.
What a concept.

Yet most days, scarcely any of us get much of a thrill from this
fact. Hang out with a few Christian types, drop the biblical truth
that they actually are a select bunch of people—a collection of royal,
God-birthed ministers, a spotless and holy group belonging to Him
(see 1 Peter 2:9-12)—and they'll argue with you! I wonder why that
might be. We, the bride of Christ, are certainly not dumb. We've
been deceived.

Try this: At church next Sunday, set up a table and hang out a
sign: "Perfect Christian Survey." Pull up a chair, whip out a note-
pad, and (if your church is big enough) ask a hundred people if they
believe that, according to a God who loves them madly, they have
become perfect. Give me your best estimate of the actual percent-
age responding, "Why, yes, I do!"

During 25 years of pastoring, I have posed that question in various ways to perhaps thousands of Christians, many of whom did not
know I was a pastor (and thus a member of the get-the-right-answer-
or-be-shamed Gestapo). My findings? Fewer than 5 percent.

Think Satan has been successful? I do too. With the lights coming on and the curtain drawing back, the Spirit (not willing that we
should live without the knowledge of how well-off we have become

with God) is revealing to us the majesty of His grace to us in Christ. Finding out all about it is in no way a trivial pursuit—it's what He wants for you.

An important first step in discovering and living with His amazing opinion of you requires a rather odd first look…a look at your death.

Questions for Discussion

1. Has the attempt to sell you on a nobility far below your own become apparent to you? How?

2. Have you been deluded into the life of a pretender? How can you tell? Are you bothered by it?

3. Have you ever thought of yourself as being holy? For what reason?

4. Would you feel uncomfortable by describing yourself as perfect? Why?

Chapter Three

You Stink!

What Does Death Have to Do with Your Life?

I have been crucified with Christ and I no longer live, but
Christ lives in me. The life I live in the body, I live by faith in
the Son of God, who loved me and gave himself for me.

GALATIANS 2:20

We cross our bridges when we come to them and
burn them behind us, with nothing to show for our
progress except a memory of the smell of smoke, and
a presumption that once our eyes watered.

TOM STOPPARD

Kneeling in prayer on a hardwood floor in Monrovia, California, in the early 1980s, I was thanking and praising God for loving me. I'm not sure why that exercise seems to produce still more of the knowledge of His affection, but it does.

As I carried on in love, I was temporarily knocked off balance when I heard the Spirit say, *Give me lust.* Well, I knew all about that. There had been many days filled with strong longings for the love of a desirable woman. A good portion of why I'd gone to school was to ogle. What better place? Most all of my friends shared in what had seemed to us a sort of sport. And if you love the sport, you play it every chance you get.

However, because I had become a Christian, I knew my ogling ways were no longer acceptable. Even though I lived in a fraternity house surrounded by sororities, and the game was on all around me, my continued participation in it repulsed me. So I drew away from the game. No dating. No lingering looks. No going to the beach. No coarse joking. No movies with even a glimpse of onscreen affection. I quit lusting. But it didn't quit me.

Because of my former expertise at the game of ogling and lust, I discovered the necessity of relational boundaries, and I drew them boldly and early. I didn't want anything to do with that powerful feeling and enticement.

So when the Holy Spirit confronted me about lust, I was at first surprised. *What do You mean?* I wondered. *I'm doing pretty well with that. I've got it under control.* Still He persisted, and I began to fear. I had come to hate what lust did and had committed myself to war against it. Anytime mutual desire reared up in new relationships with women, I made great attempts at keeping it corralled, fearing the beast within.

Give it up, son. Let Me have it.

I very nearly panicked. To let this beastly part of me back onto the field of life meant failure…ugly and awful failure. Trembling with the fear of what might happen, I stammered, "Okay," and removed my inner restraint.

Like a balloon inflated too far, too fast, I felt a sudden rush of awful desire swell my chest—only to burst and be gone. *Gone!*

Had you been walking past my little house at that moment, you'd have heard a long shout of joy rivaling the most delirious yell at a sporting event. I was ecstatic! What had happened I didn't know, but I was not the same. What the Spirit said next led me on a successful quest I want to begin to share with you. He said, *"It wasn't you."*

For weeks after that, I reveled in Christ and in a freedom I had never before experienced. I even tested it—going to classic stumbling grounds like local beaches and raucous parties. The ugly beast was gone. I prized knowing Jesus so much that subsequent relationships with women (I eventually married one of them!) took a backseat to loving and knowing Him (and rightly so). I wasn't spared from temptation, but anytime an improper thought or feeling urged me toward an improper action, I focused upon my Love, and the repulsive suggestion vanished. It couldn't find the familiar foothold in me it once had. (More about this in the next chapter.)

A verse I had known previously, which before I had not really understood, now became a secure resting place for me, explaining so much of life: "I have been crucified with Christ and I no longer live, but Christ lives in me. The life I live in the body, I live by faith in the Son of God, who loved me and gave himself for me" (Galatians 2:20).

You Already Died

To illustrate what I found, I want to ask you a question: What will have to happen in order for you to finally be free from the power of sin? If your answer is along the lines of "I'll have to die," then you're doing well. Here's one more question I'd like to ask you: As a Christian, when *did* you die? I cannot express how important the correct answer is for determining the direction and experience of your life. My own answer was faulty up until that day in Monrovia, and so was my living.

God thinks you already died—had a burial and everything. A crowd saw it all. That you may be unaware of it or that it took place long ago does not diminish the fact. Paul explained to the beleaguered Christians at Rome that they had already died as well:

> Or don't you know that all of us who were baptized into Christ Jesus were baptized into his death? We were therefore buried with him through baptism into death in order that, just as Christ was raised from the dead through the glory of the Father, we too may live a new life. If we have been united with him like this in his death, we will certainly also be united with him in his resurrection. For we know that our old self was crucified with him so that the body of sin might be done away with, that we should no longer be slaves to sin—because anyone who has died has been freed from sin (Romans 6:3-7).

Every believer has been baptized (immersed) into the death of Christ Jesus. Since many of us have seen Mel Gibson's film *The Passion of the Christ*, it's not too difficult to envision the scene at Calvary. Imagining ourselves gathered at the cross, we see Jesus "pierced for our transgressions" (Isaiah 53:5), having taken upon Himself the sins of the world as well as our full punishment. Yet, if we're to be immersed into His death, the picture in our minds must change dramatically. Somehow we've got to get where He is—more accurately, we've got to be put *into Him*.

And so, up we go. Lifted by an unseen hand, we are moved closer and closer to Him until we can see the mangled and torn body, blood streaming from His many terrible wounds. We draw so close that we can hear His tortured breathing, and, without stopping, each of us disappears into Him, immersed into Christ.

Gone.

Think of a crowd. Imagine someone in the crowd, confused and looking around, saying, "Where did Ralph go?"

"Umm…he went up there," another replies, "into Jesus. He went into Him."

"Are you sure?"

"Yeah. And now Ralph's gone. I don't think he's ever coming back either."

Gone. The same is true for you too.

When Jesus died, you died in Him too. Believers were put into Him, which means we'll never have to die for our sins or die to gain power over sin because we already died in Christ!

Certainly, it is difficult to think you have already died when there appears to be little evidence to support that reality. But I was convinced of it when kneeling on the hardwood floor in Monrovia. Because I had been a lustful ogler for years, I had not realized that I wasn't anymore, even though I had become a Christian! I kept watch over and restrained myself like a vial of nitroglycerin ready to go off at the slightest bump. With all that nervous effort, what chance did I have of discovering that the former me had been removed at the cross? I believed I was still a bomb more than I believed I had become a son, with desires and attributes in keeping with that status. I was attempting to live by faith, but what I believed wasn't true.

The Danger with "Surrender" Language

Unintentionally, we may send the false message that we haven't been included in Christ's death when we implore Christians to *surrender*. As I listened to a church radio program a while back, the speaker, citing Romans 12:1, said, "Surrendering yourself to God is the key to knowing His will for your life, and I'm embarrassed to tell you that there is so much of me not yet surrendered, not yet totally His. I want to one day get to such a point that I am not 75 percent, not 85 percent, not 95 percent, but 100 percent surrendered to Him! Then I'll be completely His!" The crowd roared an eager "Amen!"

Shaking my head, I muttered, "Ah, nuts." And in my mind came the imagined picture of several hundred listeners holding loaded pistols to their own heads. I imagined they were imploring themselves with encouraging words, such as, "See! What have I been telling you? You have to make the choice to surrender, you hard-hearted jerk! Surrender!"

If Jesus were to have walked into that room right at that moment, what do you suppose He would have said? Is that what God would say to His glorious church, crucified with Christ and chosen before the world began? "Surrender"? I don't think so.

"Surrender" means *you're not dead*, but you've been beaten by an opponent and the odds are totally against you. Then you start to think you haven't a hope, so you might as well give up. Is that what you think God is saying to you? Are you still so bad that you need to be threatened with the imaginary gun to your head, forced to give up and give in? If your surrender is what He is after, that might imply that either you are more of a dirty scoundrel than you are a holy saint, or that there are two of you, one good and godly, one bad and devilish. In either case, it's not true. You are a new you, and there's only one of you. (The next chapter is devoted almost entirely to this.)

After such a passion-filled plea to surrender, how do you suppose it's going to go for people who think that in order to please God most, we must surrender? We may for a time look good and godly, our behavior matching our zealous determination to be fully surrendered. But before long, we'll grow tired of our self-imposed vigil, our strength will wane, and sin and failure will break out all over again. And that's depressing—after all, we did it for God. Plus, working hard to keep our presumedly bad selves under the gun, we won't know anything of the grace and workings of God. Neither will we know His friendship. Does that describe you?

Believing by Agreeing

What we want is not to surrender, but to *believe*. Christians don't live primarily by being tough with themselves but by believing God has already done something tremendous! Believing in the change God has made in us will lead us to do a lot of things (like giving away our money when we could just as well purchase something with it, or serving a challenging neighbor when we could easily avoid him), but we'll do them because we believe it's now our nature to do so. We'll do them by faith in God about ourselves, agreeing with Him! No one will have to harangue us into doing something godly! In every way, acting godly and doing godly things are the most normal things we can do. Doing those things is really living. But if you don't believe you've been changed, you may not embrace your new normal. Instead, you'll need the gun to get you going. "Surrender!"

Nowhere in the new covenant is the word *surrender* used. And anytime the word *submit* is used for believers, it means that because you believe and because of what you believe, you can get under His leadership, embrace His will as your own, and find your source of life. It's found in Him—in what He did, in who He is, in where He is, and in where you are. You're in Him. You're not a stubborn, ill-mannered, nasty son or daughter of God. You're a rescued and royal son or daughter who wants to live by faith in the One who made you so. The life you're looking for doesn't come at the end of a holy gun barrel or by draping a white flag over your supposedly "sorry" self but through believing the great gospel about Him. And that's an incredibly humbling thing, and it always leads to believing the great gospel about you. If you're going to believe Him about *Him*, you've got to believe Him about *you*.

What Would Jesus Say?

Instead of using "surrender" language, I think Jesus would say to that radio audience something like this: "My wonderful brothers and sisters—I am here for you. I can see that you are fearful, and I can see that you so want to please Me. Then believe Me. You are in Me, and I am in you, just as I have said. Have I not chosen you? Have I not done everything to secure you with Me? Rest, then. Believe Me about yourselves—your worries about Me are over. You are not unclean—I have seen to it. What are you looking to do to yourselves that I have not done? What do you find insufficient? The Holy Spirit, who lives in you, will happily provide all that you need—He will see to everything. Trust Me, trust what I have done for you, and you will find rest for yourselves. I will see to it."

Oh, and drop the gun. You've already died. Wasn't one death enough?

The nature of a man predisposed to sin, "the old self," got crucified at the cross. You and I inherited a nasty nature from our distant relative Adam—a nature that was cut off from God and dead to Him. It was, however, alive to the power of sin. While sin is most often thought of as something we do or as something we fail to do, it is also (and more precisely) a power or a pressing force. Some passages in Scripture actually speak of sin as having a personality of its own.

Speaking to Cain, the Lord said, "If you do what is right, will you not be accepted? But if you do not do what is right, *sin is crouching at your door; it desires to have you,* but you must master it" (Genesis 4:7).

Paul also personified sin:

Therefore do not let sin reign in your mortal body so that you obey *its evil desires*. Do not offer the parts of your body to sin, as instruments of wickedness, but rather offer yourselves to God, as those who have been brought from death to life; and offer the parts of your body to him as instruments of righteousness (Romans 6:12-13).

We certainly feel evil desires, but they are no longer *our* evil desires. Rather, they are "*its* [sin's] evil desires." The change God made for you at the cross makes you now incompatible with sin. That plays a big part in why you feel awful after committing a sin—you're no longer a match! You don't get along with sin! After becoming a Christian, I hated lust, even if I yielded to it; *before* accepting Jesus, I was a willing participant. What a change!

That former self, dead to God but alive to sin, was killed. And you and I have received a brand-new self with the nature of a child of God. Paul explained to the Ephesians that this is why a man must be born again—he has a nature problem:

> And you were dead in your trespasses and sins, in which you formerly walked according to the course of this world, according to the prince of the power of the air, of the spirit that is now working in the sons of disobedience. Among them we too all formerly lived in the lusts of our flesh, indulging the desires of the flesh and of the mind, and were *by nature children* of wrath, even as the rest. But God, being rich in mercy, because of His great love with which He loved us, even when we were dead in our transgressions, made us alive together with Christ (by grace you have been saved), and raised us up with Him, and seated us with Him in the heavenly places in Christ Jesus, so that in the ages to come He might show the surpassing riches of His grace in kindness toward us in Christ Jesus (Ephesians 2:1-7 NASB).

The words *by nature* in verse 3 mean "by germination," or "by genetic." Our native disposition could only incur God's wrath because all we could do was satisfy the sinful cravings of our flesh, following after them. If by nature I am an ogler, what would you expect? Ogling certainly felt *natural* to me! But not after I received the new birth in Christ. Now it feels natural and delightful to do what pleases Him—we're a match! We're compatible!

God's Genes

All this is no surprise to God, who always intended to give us His genetics. God spoke to us through the prophet Ezekiel:

> I will give you a new heart and put a new spirit in you; I will remove from you your heart of stone and give you a heart of flesh. And I will put my Spirit in you and move you to follow my decrees and be careful to keep my laws (Ezekiel 36:26-27).

Because this has all taken place for you through Christ, your Father is doing something amazing concerning you—unseen and eternal. He knows you've died already and have been raised and seated in the heavenlies in Christ. So He is spreading the evidence of His work everywhere you go, successfully at all times.

Paul knew this truth well, and he proclaimed it to the Corinthians:

> But thanks be to God, who always leads us in triumphal procession in Christ and through us spreads everywhere the fragrance of the knowledge of him. For we are to God the aroma of Christ among *those who are being saved* and *those who are perishing. To the one* we are the smell of death; *to the other*, the fragrance of life. And who is equal to such a task? (2 Corinthians 2:14-16).

Following the sequence, to those who are being saved, we are the fine fragrance of death. To those who are perishing, we are the enchanting scent of life. Have you caught a whiff? When I go among fellow Christians (those who have been saved), I'm reminded that they will never have to die for their sins. That issue has been forever settled in Christ. They need not fear. But many of us have been shortchanged on our amazing security in Christ.

Furthermore, I know that we have all the power over sin we will ever need. Christians may have begun to live by sight and experience ("I sin, so I must not have power over it"), but I have terrific news: Instead of living by sight, let's live by faith—that's the way that works best. And the Holy Spirit loves it when we do! Paul knew that Christians had been crucified with Christ, and that kept him focused on who they actually were, which in turn kept his approach to them on track (1 Corinthians 2:2).

A Wonder-Inducing Fragrance

Concerning "those who are perishing," God produces from us a captivating fragrance, an otherworldly beckoning to Himself. This invisible drawing effect induces lost and confused people to wonder when they are around us. They may express that wonder strangely, but it is genuine wonder nonetheless. "You Christians live so peculiarly! Why bother, anyway?" "All you Christians care about is the Bible! *Bible* this, *Bible* that! What's the big deal?" "Don't tell me you go to church! What a waste! I quit that years ago—why haven't you?" Grudging curiosity from the lost and confused will often come at us in distorted ways, but when you consider how tragically twisted everyone is apart from the One who reverses the twist, why expect anything else? The smell of life is enchanting to them, no matter how they look when following the scent. With certainty, you may expect to see some strangely inquisitive people hanging about you.

So next time you're gathered together with a number of Christians, pay attention to what you smell. What odor will be emanating to the pleasure of the heavens? The God-glorifying scent of death.

You stink. Isn't that great?

Questions for Discussion

1. Is it challenging to think of yourself as having already died? Why?

2. Why might it be unwise to tell Christians that they need to surrender to God?

3. What happened to your old self? Why is that important?

4. What kind of nature has God given you now?

5. What fragrance is God spreading through you to nonbelievers? To believers?

Chapter Four

Who Is I?

Are You a Modification or a New Creation?

Therefore, if anyone is in Christ, he is a new creation;
the old has gone, the new has come!

2 CORINTHIANS 5:17

You can't depend on your eyes when
your imagination is out of focus.

MARK TWAIN

Living in a remote and unpopulated region of Siberia, Andrei Tol-
styk was abandoned in a crude home with the family dog by his
mother and father before his first birthday. Astonishingly, the boy
survived, and for the next seven years, his only companion was the
dog. When he was discovered by regional authorities, he was running about on all fours and growling.

Andrei faces years of difficult training in the use of speech (he
didn't know a single word), how to use utensils (he used his mouth
alone), how to accept and relate to people (he bit virtually everyone who approached him), how to use a bathroom, how and where
to sleep, and more. Doctors and psychologists are uncertain as to
whether or not Andrei can ever be taught human behavior so he can
lead a normal life. Previous attempts with other children raised in
similarly traumatic conditions provide little hope. Sadly, the under-
lying problem few have ever been able to overcome is a fundamen-
tal belief: Andrei believes he is more dog than human. Even if he
adopts the manners and customs of humans, he will do so only to

survive and fit in. Until he begins to believe what all those around him know to be true, Andrei is lost.

I believe something similar is true of many people in today's Christian community. They don't know who they are, they don't know what they have become, and so they act, all too often, in keeping with the world in which they live. While they have become the very best of this world through a new birth in Christ, having become wonderfully well-off sons and daughters of God—still, they act lost.

Knowing Who You Are

From seminars to sermons, from books to videos, we're incessantly instructing each other on how to live right. Fathers should act kindly and kingly, and here's how. Mothers should be compassionate and capable, and here's how. Employees should be conscientious and diligent, and bosses should be fair and insightful, and here's how. And the reason? Because God wants you to, that's why. That's how you can obey Him and please Him. But that's not really why.

Raised in a pagan world, we've been rescued and made actual sons and daughters of God through the Lord Jesus. If now we attempt to act like Him while being unaware we've been *made* like Him, or if we adopt the manners and customs of Christ in order to "survive and fit in," we'll be just like Andrei—still off track, even if we have the right look. From fathers and mothers, to brothers and sisters, to bosses and employees, we don't act the way we should because we don't know who we are. Further, we don't know who we are not.

You Are Not Your Worst Enemy

Considering the astounding change God has made in us, it's to His glory that we find out about it. It will be helpful to uncover any deceptions that might now be hindering your belief, so let me ask you a question: How often do you think any of the following things about yourself? *I am such an idiot. I'll never get anything right. I always do the worst thing.* And my personal favorite: *I'm my own worst enemy.*

Most, if not all of us, have had these kinds of thoughts before believing in Jesus as well as after believing, but with one significant difference: After believing in Jesus, our standards for behavior increased dramatically, as did our corresponding potential for failure.

Think of it. Were your standards of behavior—your expectations of how you should and would treat people and situations—higher *before* receiving Christ or *after?* Do you live up to those standards? If not, what's your problem? Many Christians think one of two things: It might be the devil, but more than likely, it's me—I'm the problem. "*I!*"

So, here's the follow-up question I'd like you to ask yourself: Who *is* I? And if you're struggling to come up with a definitive answer at this moment, you're not alone. In fact, you're in good company. See if the way Paul wrestled with this makes sense to you. To the Christians at Rome, Paul wrote:

> For what I am doing, I do not understand; for I am not practicing what I would like to do, but I am doing the very thing I hate. But if I do the very thing I do not want to do, I agree with the Law, confessing that the Law is good. So now, no longer am I the one doing it, but sin which dwells in me. For I know that nothing good dwells in me, that is, in my flesh; for the willing is present in me, but the doing of the good is not. For the good that I want, I do not do, but I practice the very evil that I do not want. But if I am doing the very thing I do not want, I am no longer the one doing it, but sin which dwells in me. I find then the principle that evil is present in me, the one who wants to do good. For I joyfully concur with the law of God in the inner man, but I see a different law in the members of my body, waging war against the law of my mind and making me a prisoner of the law of sin which is in my members. Wretched man that I am! Who will set me free from the body of this death? Thanks be to

God through Jesus Christ our Lord! So then, on the one
hand I myself with my mind am serving the law of God,
but on the other, with my flesh the law of sin (Romans
7:15-25 NASB).

It's not difficult to hear Paul's anguish, and it's somehow com-
forting to know we're not alone in this wrestling with self. The first
nine words of this passage sum up a lot of my life! Indeed, most
of us are rightly intrigued with our behavior…especially when it's
monstrous.

The Monster Inside

Several years ago, my wife and I took our daughters to Disney-
land. As we were thoroughly enjoying our day in the park, we met
up with some friends who had children the same ages as ours. They
had just been on one of the scariest and most exhilarating rides—the
Matterhorn—and approached us with lots of whooping and carrying
on, inviting us to join them on another go of it. Both of our daughters had heard plenty of screaming coming from terrified people on
that ride, having walked past it several times earlier in the day. Ellen,
our older child, cast a wary look at the ride and said, "I don't think so.
No." Our three-year-old Emma positively sparkled and said, "Yeah!"

The looks my wife and I exchanged meant that we were searching for our own opinion, as well as giving the Holy Spirit a moment
to weigh in on the issue. Both of us sensed a sort of green light, and
so off we went.

Meandering through the serpentine line gave me plenty of time
to tell Emma what to expect. Darting roller-coaster cars caught her
eyes, and the shrieks coming from the occupants filled the night
air, making her eyes wild with delighted expectation and cautious
apprehension. Finally our turn came.

When once we were fastened in with Emma securely nestled in
my lap, I began to calmly and confidently narrate our progress. As
on most roller coasters, we began by going up and up and up into
the darkness of the mountain, which meant we were very soon to

come *down*. At the instant of our descent, Emma let out a low "*Ehh-hhhhhhhhhhhhhhhhhh!*" which she never stopped, except to get a breath to start it over again. "*Ehhhhhhhhhhhhhhhhhhh!*" she said, as we zigged and zagged violently through the black, occasionally whizzing out into the night air, only to whiz back inside. I did the fatherly thing and encouraged her at virtually every moment: "Isn't this great, Emma! We're doing fine—really good!" All she said was, "*Ehhhhhhhhhhhhhhhhhhhh!*"

But even though I had ridden this ride many years before, I had forgotten one thing. Halfway through the ride, and after rounding a turn, the biggest, baddest, nastiest, overgrown, white gorilla with red, laser beam eyes clawed and roared at us from a ledge just above our path. At once, "*Ehhhhhhhhhhhhhhhhhhhh!*" changed dramatically to a much higher and much louder, "*Aaaaaaaaaaaaaaaaaaaay!*" The abominable snowman I had forgotten was suddenly Emma's terrible monster. Even though I poured into her ear daddy assurances that it was fake and harmless, it took a few turns before "*Aaaaaaaaaaa-aaaaaaaaay!*" turned again into a more subdued, "*Ehhhhhhhhhhh-hhhhhhhh!*"

But I had forgotten one more thing—there were two of them! Terror returned and Emma's pitch and volume shot right back up again. It wasn't until we neared the end of the ride that she returned to her more normal state of agitation.

Drawing her limp, octopus-like body from the car and having visions of years of therapy for a traumatized Emma, I heard her ask softly, "What's the monster doing now, Daddy? What's he doing?"

Suddenly hoping the scars wouldn't be all that enduring, I said, "Well, he's not real, you know, but he's probably waving his arms and doing that roar thing as other unsuspecting people whiz by. But remember, he's not real. He's just a machine."

And those two words which made my blood pressure go down—"Okay, Daddy"—rang sweetly from my daughter. Ah, success…except that she asked, "What's the monster doing now, Daddy?" at least two dozen more times before finally falling asleep on the drive home. No matter my answer—and I had what I thought were some really good ones—she was captivated by the thought of the monster, and it wouldn't let her go.

I'm sure most parents teach their children pretty well about monsters, whether imagined (such as Mr. Abominable) or real (such as dangerous animals or people). We're understandably concerned with monsters. But I'm not so sure we teach our children about the monster they need to know about far more than any other—*the monster within*. Paul had one, and you and I do too. Like all monsters, this one is terrible and dangerous, making us feel and do hideous things.

In our passage from Romans 7, what was Paul's biggest problem? Wasn't it doing? Look at verses 17-21. In the NIV, the little word *do* appears 20 times! (And that is not even counting the occurrences of *does* and *doing*!) Concerning our behavior, one might say this is where the rubber meets the road. In all the admonitions concerning the behavior of the believer, this is perhaps the most foundational passage in the New Testament.

We know our behavior, feelings, and thought life aren't what they ought to be. So what's our problem? Regarding growing up in Christ, here's the point: As a Christian, you must believe that *you* are not the problem, but *something in you* is. Paul wrote that when he sinned, it was no longer him who did it (Romans 7:17,20). How can that be? Either he was an arrogant cop-out artist with an amazing flair for denial, or he knew what he was talking about. And it wasn't him who sinned. If we ask *where* Paul's problem lay, we begin to understand what led him toward sin. His problem was in his "flesh" (Romans 7:18 NASB). Nothing good lived there! In fact, sin lived in Paul's flesh. Paul's problem wasn't with himself—after all, Jesus had crucified that former self and made him new (as we saw in chapter 3). Paul's problem was with what *wasn't* crucified—his flesh.

The flesh is a monster, producing monstrous thoughts and feelings, monstrous attitudes, and monstrous behavior! It will never change. One can never train it up or educate it and expect it to act anything but monstrous. But neither Paul nor you nor I *are the flesh*. We *have* flesh, and at times it *has* us, but we are not the flesh!

For a long time, that's what we were, but not anymore. Jesus made a historic change.

Where It All Began

From that terrible day when Adam and Eve passed through the gates of the paradise—Eden—and began their lives in a comparative wasteland, man has become well acquainted with flesh. Having been born into a dependent, life-giving relationship with God, Adam and Eve were blessed with many of the qualities and characteristics that made up the image of God (see Genesis 1:26-28). With the life of God as his life, man was to steward the Garden surroundings as God would. But when Adam and Eve chose to do things differently, independently, they were banished to a quasi-life of independence from God, an existence without real life.

God is life—its very source. Everything He does erupts with life. When Adam and Eve were expelled from the Garden, they were separated from life and left to do what they could with what they had left—mortal flesh. Those first steps on the other side of the gate were the initial stumbling of empty mankind. Imagine that first night outside the Garden for Adam and Eve, newly separated from God and without life for the first time. *Terrifying* would be an understatement.

The shocking realization of what they lost has echoed throughout history, requiring every relative of Adam and Eve to make something of living *without life*, to make a fallen existence work. But no matter how good a functioning man or woman looks, regardless of what they do for their kids and their community or how well they plan for their retirement, they are without life—they are dust.

Speaking to Adam and Eve and to all who come after them, God said, "By the sweat of your brow you will eat your food until you return to the ground, since from it you were taken; for dust you are and to dust you will return" (Genesis 3:19). Quoting the psalmist,

Paul explains the wretched state of man to the Romans: "As it is written: 'There is no one righteous, not even one; there is no one who understands, no one who seeks God. All have turned away, they have together become worthless; there is no one who does good, not even one'" (Romans 3:10-12; see also Psalm 14:1-3; 53:1-3).

"*Worthless.*" "*Not even one.*" Ouch. It's not easy to admit, is it?

Try posting "You and I Are Worthless" as a bumper sticker on your car (or maybe on your neighbors') and see what happens! With centuries of practice, it is now common for men and women to live by the flesh and call it normal—it's all they know because it's all they have. As we've seen, it makes us prey for a terrible and trivial pursuit. But get alone with someone and they might admit that life is totally unsatisfying and empty—it doesn't work. You and I know the reason: Having been designed for something more, all they have is *flesh.* They're left to walking "in the futility of their mind, being darkened in their understanding, excluded from the life of God" (Ephesians 4:17-18 NASB). No one can live like that. But many of us try—even Christians.

As it was with Adam and Eve outside the gates of Eden, *the flesh* is that part of us that suggests a course for living that results in living without the life of God. Although God lives inside the Christian, living by the flesh means *life without guts.* It's *gutless* because God isn't in it—there's no divine power involved.

How does it happen? Let's take a look.

The Soul—Perceiving and Expressing

Each of us has a soul. The soul is what I like to call our *perceiver-expresser*—it feels and thinks, and it knows what's going on all the time. And it looks for a way of expression. When you turn on the television, walk into a room full of people, or hear the phone ring, you'll be instantly alert and aware—your perceiver is doing what it does. Your soul *perceives* something, and you feel fear, happiness, sorrow, calm—any number of things. Following the feeling is the need to make some type of expression. You'll think, *I'd better do something.*

At that point, your perceiver-expresser searches for input, and your flesh quickly suggests an expressive action—*here's what to do*—often with thoughts and feelings to match. The flesh is all about action (output). It disregards the presence of the Holy Spirit in you, and it also ignores the fact that you are now a spirit. It runs right by you and speaks to your soul: *Get moving!*

And that's where the danger lurks. If you don't believe that your "insides" are vastly different than they were before you were born again, your soul will connect with your flesh, and the outcome or *deeds of the flesh* will express living without God. Even though He lives in you, He won't be involved. The kingdom of God now in you will be powerless and life will be *gutless*. It will be by the flesh and not by the Spirit.

Adam and Eve most likely never grew accustomed to living by the flesh (living without God's life) and were likely haunted all of their days by the memory of living connected to God. But centuries later, you and I have never known even the haunting, so the desire for true life must come another way.

It might go something like this: Your perceiver-expresser notices you've gained weight, and the thought that follows is that you're not successful because you're fat. Right on cue, the flesh offers condemning thoughts: *You knew this would happen, fatso!* If you listen to that for more than a few seconds, the flesh will suggest a course of action: *Well, you'll never change, so go ahead and eat a gallon of ice cream! Might as well have a little pleasure since you won't have it any other way!* And if there's any ice cream in the freezer, it's a goner. Or the flesh might suggest, *Buy some workout clothes, get back in the gym, and get going! You really can't live until you get thin…but you can do it if you make it your new crusade.*

Following your ice-cream binge, you may feel depression, shame, or even rage, and you might swear you'll never do it again. Or, in the second example, you may feel a rush of motivation and buy a new wardrobe. Either way, the flesh is having its way with you because God isn't involved in the expression of your life. He's got nothing to do. To be clear, you're not sinning, but neither are you living as you might.

The Holy Spirit to the Rescue

Fortunately, that won't work for long. Since you've been born again and redesigned by God, you now crave what you've never known—God's life. The Holy Spirit will put up a fuss and alert you. You'll feel conflict, as if you're just not getting all that you can out of your Christian walk. And that's true because you're not getting real life. We'll look intently at this in the next few chapters, but the new way of living means that you look to the Spirit in you and *He* produces the life. In this instance, the Holy Spirit is also about output. The Bible calls His output *the fruit of the Spirit* (Galatians 5:22-23). When He is at work in you, when you listen and follow His leading, the expression of your soul will be godly.

Now while you don't always have to wait for the flesh to exert itself before listening for the Spirit, you probably will to begin with. That's okay because you're just waking up to the desire and need of another way of living—you'll get there! So if, after hearing the suggestion of the flesh concerning your weight, you instead turn to the Spirit, you might hear something like this: *It's all right, you know. We can walk together in this little thing. Let's make it something for us to do together. Your life is with me—remember? And I never measure you by the scale—it's not accurate. But I will satisfy you, and we'll be together.* Living in this way, you may feel genuine peace, love, and assurance. Depression and shame will be gone because the life of God will be working in you. The expression that comes through you will make that apparent. You'll have God's life for your life.

That's how important the soul is. It perceives what goes on around (accurately or inaccurately) and then expresses what goes on inside. What your perceiver-expresser feels and thinks is not really the problem, so much as what happens because of it—the expression. If you, a spirit-child of God, choose to follow the suggestion of the flesh, you will express the behavior of the flesh—you'll be a fleshly

Christian, at least in that moment. You will have returned to the life you lived when you were gutless, when God did not yet live in you. If, on the other hand, you choose to live by faith and offer yourself to the Holy Spirit now in you, you will express the activity of the Spirit—you'll be a Spirit-led and Spirit-filled Christian. No longer gutless.

Whatever your soul perceives is no longer the problem area of your life. You don't validate your walk with God if you're having good thoughts and feelings, and you don't invalidate your walk if you're having bad thoughts and feelings. That's not the point! Your starting point is not feelings, but spirit—the Holy Spirit in union with your spirit. Beginning with that truth, your experience and expression will be influenced by His life.

And that's life—*real* life.

Be Who You Are, Not Who You Were

Through Christ, you and I have been given God's life with a new way to live. Since Jesus, "the way, the truth and *the life*," made His entrance into us, we're not flesh anymore! Jesus has successfully made us spirit, new creations now filled with God, now filled with *life!* Remember? That's why He came in the first place, to give us life (John 10:10; 1 John 5:12).

We know who we were and what we were born—pagan-natured flesh bags—but we also know who we are and what we were born a *second* time: godly-natured spirits, sons and daughters designed for life. What a miracle.

You and I know that while we still have a monster (flesh) and can walk in the manner of a monster (by the flesh), we are not monsters! We have an enemy, but we are not enemies of God; the enemy is not us. God has a problem, but it is not us. We are not God's problem anymore. If we believe we are the problem, if we believe we are the reason for our stumbling and for our sinning against God and against each other, we are deceived. (And the natural course of deception is that we're off course but don't know it.) We'll usually make war on sin, which, in our thinking, usually means we make war on ourselves. For example, if I think I'm the problem, then where do my attention and my efforts go? Right at me...or the "me" I think I am. And that forces me into a double life. You too.

Luther Price wrote, "Be what you is, not what you ain't; 'cause if you ain't what you is, you is what you ain't." In other words, if you believe you are something (the flesh) when, in fact, you are not, the life you live will be a false one. You won't live as you really are and have become because you'll believe you're something else. You'll live as you ain't.

This is why we should not implore Christians to *surrender* but rather encourage them to *believe*. While it's true that we carry the flesh, that isn't us. Neither does it surrender to God's commands. Paul summed this up nicely in his letter to the Romans:

> The mind set on the flesh is hostile toward God; for it does not subject itself to the law of God, for it is not even able to do so; and those who are in the flesh cannot please God. However, *you are not in the flesh but in the Spirit*, if indeed the Spirit of God dwells in you. But if anyone does not have the Spirit of Christ, he does not belong to Him (Romans 8:7-9 NASB).

Now that you have been reborn and belong to God, "*you are not in the flesh*"! You're no longer found there! You're "in the Spirit"! And you're *of* the Spirit!

This is why (falsely identifying ourselves) whenever we implore ourselves to surrender, we add fuel to the false fight! If we believe that the part of us that seems stubborn and reluctant to offer itself to God *is us*, then we've believed the flesh is us, and we'll try to command its surrender. Yikes! No wonder we can never seem to do it. "Now, look here, flesh—*I'm serious!* I've had it with you and your terrible rule in my life, so I'm ordering you to cease your efforts immediately. You must no longer produce all that lousy, ugly stuff you've long pumped into my life—*no more of that!* Further, you must submit to daily prayer and Bible reading and *like it!* You hear me? *Surrender!* I mean it!"

Twisted in our belief, we will invariably be twisted in our efforts. The way out of the distortion is to live by faith and rightly identify the monster. Paul said that if he sinned, it was not him sinning. Who was it? The monster! The flesh—that which Paul used to be but was no longer, ever since he had been remade and given life.

Here's the promise of God and the direction for your new life:

> But if the Spirit of Him who raised Jesus from the dead dwells in you, He who raised Christ Jesus from the dead will also give *life* to your mortal bodies through His Spirit who dwells in you. So then, brethren, we are under obligation, not to the flesh, to live according to the flesh—for if you are living according to the flesh, you must die; but if by the Spirit you are putting to death the deeds of the body, you will live. For all who are being led by the Spirit of God, these are sons of God (Romans 8:11-14 NASB).

You're no monster—you're a newly made child of God! You have the Spirit of God, and you have *life*. Because this is so, you may now happily put to death the ugly and awful deeds of the flesh. (More about that in chapter 5.)

Don't Misidentify the Source of Bad Behavior

When sin is evident in your life, it isn't the evidence that you are still seriously sinister, nor is it what you truly want to do. Sin is now a fleshly compulsion through the mental and emotional faculties of your body to reenact those empty days of long ago by rejecting dependence upon God in order to do something else. Empty stumbling. Living without guts. Your perceiver-expresser has gone haywire.

Now what do we do with this? If I offend you, I'll say something like, "I'm sorry I did that to you." But I'll know where it came from (the flesh). Of course, if I don't own the offense and apologize to you, I'm irresponsible, and our relationship will be impaired. After all, the behavior came through me—I'm responsible. However, if I do not accurately identify the producer of the behavior, I'll be blaming the wrong thing, most likely the devil or me, and I'll be boxing the air.

So, when you feel as if you want to deceive, where does it come from? When you feel anger coming on, where does it come from? When you feel a desire to scream profanities, where does it come from? When you feel lust, when you feel like avoiding the Spirit's leading, when you feel as if you want to jump into sarcasm in order to avoid the depths of truth, where does that stuff come from? Not from you. However, the monster is very good at masquerading as you, making you think the flesh is you. What a lie that is!

If we think there was, in fact, no death, no crucifixion with Christ of the former *us* on the inside (the predisposed-to-sin, children-of-wrath-by-nature *us*), then, believing the lie, we will continually attempt to correct ourselves, straighten ourselves up, make something out of ourselves, *do something to change ourselves*. And we'll think God wants us to as well. The implication? He hasn't changed us, and we're not children of His! We may have the title "son" or "daughter," but we don't have the nature—we don't have the genetics.

The Old "I" Is Dead

As long as we believe the lie that the old "I" still lives at the center of our being, the apostle Paul's words will have no meaning and no power in our lives—"I have been crucified with Christ and I no longer live" (Galatians 2:20). Believing the lie, tragically, we're set up to work against our new, real, actual son-or-daughter-of-God selves. But Peter gives us the incredible truth:

> His divine power has given us everything we need for life and godliness through our knowledge of him who called us by his own glory and goodness. Through these

he has given us his very great and precious promises, so
that through them *you may participate in the divine nature*
and escape the corruption in the world caused by evil
desires (2 Peter 1:3-4).

That beautiful italicized phrase means that you and I have become actual partakers or sharers of the divine genetic. After your
new birth in Christ, what delighted you was different, and what
grieved you was unlike what saddened you before. You discovered
new desires ("I want to read the Bible!"), new delights ("I enjoy worshiping God!"), and new sorrows ("I so dislike sin!") because you
received a new nature with desires, delights, and sorrows to match.
You've been regerminated! I don't know why we talk to each other
as if we don't want to do the will of God now—we do!

The apostle John writes, "Yet to all who received him, to those
who believed in his name, he gave the right to become children *of*
God—children born not of natural descent, nor of human deci-
sion or a husband's will, but born *of* God" (John 1:12-13). Those
final three words—*born of God*—literally mean "out of God were
birthed." Christians have been born *of* God, not simply *by* God, and
may now take part and involve themselves in Him. We're compatible! We've been given a new nature with the genetic code of God
Himself, who has birthed us all over again, birthed us of Himself.

More than likely, you'll not always feel that you're living up to
your genetic connection, but the facts will never be altered. What
the Bible says is true of you *is* true of you whether you feel it or not.

However, that's precisely where your enemy, the devil, will aim
his attack. His method will be to induce you to pay particular attention to your feelings, behavior, and thought life, and he will tempt
you to label those things as more indicative of who you are than of
who the Bible says you are. If he can get you to believe you are what
you feel, do, and think about, then the devil will have deceived you.
He will have moved you away from the *truth* about you found in
the gospel:

> Once you were alienated from God and were enemies in
> your minds because of your evil behavior. But now he has
> reconciled you by Christ's physical body through death
> to present you holy in his sight, without blemish and free
> from accusation—if you continue in your faith, estab-
> lished and firm, *not moved* from the hope held out in the
> gospel (Colossians 1:21-23).

God did all the reconciling necessary even when we were His
enemies, even when we were dead in our transgressions (see also
Ephesians 2:4-5). In doing so, He made us entirely new and pure
and completely free from flaw. Flawless! How could sons and daughters of His be less? And He made us to be free from accusation *as long
as we do not move from our great hope in the gospel*! But if we move
away, preferring to take our identity from what we see and feel, what
will happen to us? We'll no longer be free from the allegations of the
enemy, and instead, we'll get beat up all day long. It will only stop
when somehow we're put back into our right mind, believing again
what God has done for us and to us in Christ Jesus.

Paul writes, "Therefore, if anyone is in Christ, he is *a new creation*; the old has gone, the new has come!" (2 Corinthians 5:17).
The two Greek words for *new creation* do not mean that we got an
upgrade (more RAM for our inner computer) or that our slate was
wiped clean for a time. No, we have been made an entirely new,
original formation. The moment before our new birth we were one
thing (a child of wrath by nature), and the moment following, we
became brand-new, unique children of God by nature. Yet, if we
don't know it, we might not look for who we have become and
instead believe we're not all that different…we're just supposed to
do different things now. But that's not true.

So, if you have been busily trying everything you can to make
the old you go, you've been deceived into fighting a war that is not
taking place. The old you *did* go. If, because of what you see and feel,
you've been trying everything you can to make the new you come,

you have also been deceived into fighting a nonexistent battle. The new you *did* come. You have a monster, but you are no monster. You're a son or daughter of God.

And that's the answer to the question "Who is 'I'?"—I am a child of God.

Questions for Discussion

1. Why is it that many Christians act so, well, un-Christianly?

2. What are some common thoughts you've had about yourself in your life?

3. Why is it important to identify the *flesh*?

4. Why is it important to identify the soul, your *perceiver-expresser*?

5. When sin is evident in your life, are you the problem?

Chapter Five

The Demolition Derby

Why Do You Feel Like a Crash-test Dummy?

What a wretched man I am! Who will rescue me from this body
of death? Thanks be to God—through Jesus Christ our Lord!

ROMANS 7:24-25

The art of living is more like that of wrestling than of dancing; the
main thing is to stand firm and be ready for an unseen attack.

MARCUS AURELIUS

Okay, I admit it—I can be dramatic. I don't understand how
people can live seemingly unaffected day to day: a little smile
here, a little frown there, a bit of excitement now and again, and
perhaps a momentary little lapse or two into demonstrated anger. I
don't get that. Maybe I just do it bigger…me and Texas.

But I know they must feel the same battle going on within them
that I do every day. I can feel peaceful and secure one moment,
tumultuous and frail the next. I can feel loving and loved, and in
about a nanosecond, a sudden surge into the heat of hatred has me
rolling my eyes and gasping for air. You know that battle?

Wow. What a cacophony of confusing thoughts and feelings
goes on in me. If I'm truly a vessel of God, I must be a broken-
down, leaky little rowboat, worthy only to putter around the bay!
You too? What's wrong with us? Too much television? Too much sec-
ular music? Too much politics? (Well, yes, but that's another story.)
Why is there such a battle within? I try hard to have good thoughts
and feelings, but the opposite of what I want and like seems ever to

crash into me like a sudden car wreck! Why do I seem to have an everyday demolition derby going on inside of me, banging around on my inner racetrack? Does it mean I'm not doing very well as a Christian?

On the contrary, it's a really good sign. If you and I will pay attention, allowing the inner conflict to do something for us, we'll see incredible results and miraculous outcomes. Bear with me for a bit.

Who Are the Players?

Most dramas I enjoy have more than one player, and interaction between the characters is what it's all about. I don't want resolution alone in my drama either. I also want journey, battle, sorrow, meaning—and triumph. Every single day of our lives, that's what's going on in a drama played out within us.

Notice carefully the players in the following passage from the apostle Paul:

> Walk by the Spirit [player 1], and you [player 2] will not carry out the desire of the flesh [player 3]. For the flesh [3] sets its desire against the Spirit [1], and the Spirit [1] against the flesh [3]; for these [1 and 3] are in opposition to one another, so that you [2] may not do the things that you please. But if you [2] are led by the Spirit [1], you are not under the Law (Galatians 5:16-18 NASB).

So here's the question: In our little drama, who are you? Are you player 1? No one's confused about that—obviously, you're not the Holy Spirit. Are you player 3? Negative. You and I have what the Bible calls "flesh" (something that we'll always have and that produces awful thoughts and feelings all by itself), but *we are not* the flesh. You picked player 2, right?

You're not the Spirit, and you're not the flesh—you're you. (Hang in there…) If you're player 2, where are players 1 and 3, and who is having the fight? If you answered, "They're in me, and *they're* having the fight!" go to the head of the class—you've got it! The two of them, the Spirit and the flesh, are having a no-holds-barred brawl on the course of your inner oval! (See? Car racing really *is* from God!) And each is looking for a devastating angle that will win the race.

From your seat within the arena, will you ever be able to resolve their conflict? Perhaps bring out the yellow flag and send them to the pits? Or usher them to the bargaining table? Maybe convince them to give a little for the good of both teams? Or introduce mutually agreed upon equipment modifications and restrictions? No. Not ever. *Never.*

If the high goal of your life has been to reduce or restrict inner conflict, as if that were the primary godly battle, then even while feeling the struggle within, there is much kept from you because you've been engaged in the wrong race.

If you and I believe that the conflict within is *our* conflict, we'll marshal virtually every resource we have and wage war over something we cannot resolve. Though we join the right side and employ proper tactics (prayer, Bible reading, fasting, and so on) and even have seasonal conferences or strategy sessions, putting into play offensives designed to finally provide the triumph for which we've been fighting, that crazy conflict keeps happening anyway. The longer we fight the battle that way, the more evidence there is that we're not actually winning anything. We're not taking any of the enemy's turf, nor are we plundering his strongholds. And eventually, we may even join the great number of people who have lost the desire to battle anymore.

Knowing God Makes Us Victorious

Behind the scenes of the struggle, we wonder why we can't end this turmoil we're having. Why does it seem to flare up at the oddest moments? Why don't the victories last? And that ugly thought often running amok through our thinking will secure our focus: *What's wrong with me?*

Sleepless nights and tumultuous days teach us all that inner turmoil is indeed terrible, and something must be done about it. But having become sons and daughters of God, the weapons of our warfare are not at all the same as those of people who are not yet sons and daughters of God. *Neither are our goals.* We're not simply human anymore—we mustn't fight as if we still were! The battle is for a prize more valuable than anything of this earth. It belongs to us and is worth a ferocious fight.

History shows that few kings enter battle just to battle. Something else—something valuable—makes the fight worth it. If they had more land, more crops, or more slaves, they could be more and do more, and they could have more influence. Ever-expanding territory is the evidence of their power and wisdom on display, and it is often the goal they seek. Everyone involved knows it's not about the war; it's about the results. And so they fight. That's what the fight within is all about—*results.*

The problem isn't the skirmish itself. The attack is upon our knowing God *in that very moment.* That's what the battle is about—knowing God! And that's what is worth our every effort. Having already been secured for eternity in Christ, we battle to know God in the midst of the danger and turmoil, allowing for Him who is within us to be active! What we want is to know Him in the fight so He can do something about it. We're given over to a battle within "so that the life of Jesus may also be revealed in our body" (2 Corinthians 4:10).

Short of salvation, God's greatest gift to us is that we may know Him who now lives within us. It's not difficult to imagine that nearly every battle we encounter, nearly every strategy taken by the enemy is viciously targeting that gift…as well as the result of the gift! And that's why we fight. (More about that in the next chapter.)

Paul was no stranger to the battle within:

> For though we walk in the flesh, we do not war according to the flesh, for the weapons of our warfare are not of the flesh, but divinely powerful for the destruction of fortresses. We are destroying speculations and every lofty thing raised up *against the knowledge of God*, and we are

taking every thought captive to the obedience of Christ
(2 Corinthians 10:3-5 NASB).

Certainly Paul didn't mean the bookish knowledge of God, which
we are to tuck into our minds for later reference, but the right-now
knowing of God, the Warrior beyond defeat! Paul advocated warfare against any and every fleshly incursion into our thoughts that
might hinder our knowing God. That is the fleshly enemy tactic—
to prevent them from knowing Him. Why? As they do, the holy evidence of Christ will overwhelm the twisted evidence of the flesh.

Let the First Player Take Control

When the demolition derby begins banging around within, that's
when God shows up in us. How? In the conflict, in light of the brawl,
you (player 2) make a thoughtful, believing *choice*.

Galatians 5:16-17 tells us that when we live by the Spirit and are
being led by the Spirit, we will not succumb to the seduction of the
flesh or carry out its influential leading. Both the Spirit (player 1)
and the flesh (player 3) *are influencers toward behavior,* and we are
the recipients of that influence. The flesh attempts to influence you
(player 2) in order that it may express itself through your soul, the
perceiver-expresser of your life. And what are its actions? How does
it behave?

> The deeds [the behavior] of the flesh [player 3] are evident
> [and, oh, how you'll feel them!], which are: immorality,
> impurity, sensuality, idolatry, sorcery, enmities, strife, jeal-
> ousy, outbursts of anger, disputes, dissensions, factions,
> envying, drunkenness, carousing, and things like these
> (Galatians 5:19-21 NASB).

How about that? Seen any of that stuff around your house lately?
As you roll your eyes in recognition, consider this: Who's acting?
Who's misbehaving? Player 2? No. Player 3, Mr. Flesh, is misbehav-
ing through you, player 2. It feels awful, and it should—you lost the

fight, and the evidence is obvious…and twisted. You've been violated and abused.

Oh yes, in the end, you're responsible. But did the real you, the
actual you, the one born brand-new, the new creation, son-or-
daughter-of-God-by-nature *you* do it? No! It came *through you*. In
the battle, you fell under the influence, and you did nasty, naughty
stuff. But was it you? No, it came through you, and your perceiver-
expresser (your soul) put it on display.

That's why the apostle Paul said in his letter to the Roman church
regarding foul, sinful behavior plaguing him, "Now if I do what I
do not want to do, *it is no longer I who do it,* but it is sin living in me
that does it" (Romans 7:20). Paul knew what we must know: *There
are three players in the drama.* Two players (1 and 3) vie for influence
leading to feelings and acts, while one player (2) follows the leader,
and out comes the action revealing the influence. See?

The apostle came to know that it wasn't up to him to produce
feelings and desires leading to certain behaviors. *That wasn't and
isn't the game!* Because we have been made vessels for God in which
the demolition derby drama is at all times possible, our role is not
to produce what goes on inside but to choose sides and *give ourselves* to the Spirit. He will then see to the outcome, and express
Himself through us in godly feelings and behaviors. That's when
God's behavioral requirements are "fulfilled *in us* who do not walk
according to the flesh [player 3] but according to the Spirit [player
1]" (Romans 8:4 NKJV). It's a perfectly astounding fit!

And what can we (player 2) expect the influence of the Holy
Spirit to be in the midst of the battle? What will the feelings and
behavior coming through us look like and feel like if we offer ourselves to Him (player 1), right in that moment?

> But the fruit of the Spirit is love, joy, peace, patience,
> kindness, goodness, faithfulness, gentleness, self-control;
> against such things there is no law. Now those who belong
> to Christ Jesus have crucified the flesh with its passions

and desires. *If we live by the Spirit, let us also walk by the Spirit* (Galatians 5:22-25 NASB).

Can you imagine Him produced in you? His feelings, His ability, His likes manifested in you? What would be better than that? It feels right too, and it should—you've been made for this.

How do we see Him formed in us? How may we have this delight? We'll look intently into that in a couple of chapters, but first it will be enormously helpful to see how it has been kept from you, how old and awful flesh behaviors have seemingly been resurrected and given new life. It's crazy, isn't it?

As a prelude to what's ahead, read a summarizing, three-sentence passage from know-it-all Paul:

> Therefore do not let sin reign in your mortal body so that you [player 2] obey its [player 3's] evil desires. Do not offer the parts of your body to sin, as instruments of wickedness, but rather offer yourselves to God [player 1], as those who have been brought from death to life; and offer the parts of your body to him as instruments of righteousness. For sin shall not be your master, because you are not under law, but under grace (Romans 6:12-14).

That's how grace works, and it's especially effective for the demolition derby drama. You're set up for it and you're better off than you think.

Questions for Discussion

1. How have you felt the conflict between flesh and Spirit in you?

2. Describe your thoughts and feelings upon finding out that it's not your conflict but theirs.

3. How much time and effort have you given to inner-conflict resolution?

4. How does it make you feel to know that the goal of life isn't to make yourself better or to resolve inner turmoil, but to know God?

Chapter Six

He Ain't Heavy

Holy Spirit—Life of the Party

If the ministry that condemns men is glorious, how much
more glorious is the ministry that brings righteousness!

2 CORINTHIANS 3:9

A story to me means a plot where there is some
surprise. Because that is how life is—full of surprises.

ISAAC BASHEVIS SINGER

Speaking at a church not long ago, I surprised the congregation
with a pop quiz. "Where is God?" I asked.

"He's everywhere!" someone offered, a confident look on her
face.

Scanning the crowd, a good number of people looked as though
they wondered why I didn't already know that. *We're in big trouble,*
they might have thought.

"Okay, right," I continued. "But where is He most happy to be
at this moment? Where does He enjoy being most?"

A young man in the middle of the crowd offered tentatively, "In
me?"

"Yes! Bingo!" I replied. "And here's the follow-up question: What's
He doing in there? Right now, what does He feel like?" Tough question.

Most of us do not often think about "*God in me,*" but about "*God
out there.*" It seems almost preposterous to think of "God in me,"
and it has been this way for a long time, even in the day of Jesus.

> Once, having been asked by the Pharisees when the king-
> dom of God would come, Jesus replied, "The kingdom
> of God does not come with your careful observation, nor
> will people say, 'Here it is,' or 'There it is,' because the
> kingdom of God is within you" (Luke 17:20-21).

I have often wondered what it will be like when I set foot into the realm where Jesus reigns, where God is obviously present and does all that He pleases. Miraculously, that place is inside of me and inside of you right now. If it's true that "Christ in you" is your hope of glory (Colossians 1:27) and your expectation of incredible things and God-birthed successes in this life, then we want to be on alert and responsive to Him in us right now.

God's at Work in You

God made His home in you and me, and He would love to be busy there. I think God is more interested in what goes on in me than in what goes on around me. And I think that's where most of His work goes on—in me. More than working on things around me, I think *I'm* His work. *Me*. I'm God's work for today, and so are you.

Notice the first five words of the following verse: "*For we are God's workmanship*, created in Christ Jesus to do good works, which God prepared in advance for us to do" (Ephesians 2:10).

As it has been with me, I suspect it has been with you. We're focused on what goes on around us, tailoring ourselves to make life go as well as we can manage. When life around us goes only so-so (or worse!), so goes our prayer life. And so go our expectations of how God works.

But I think we're looking for God to work in an area that is way down on His priority list. Christians are His primary work. Working within them! I believe that's what bothered Paul the most about the Galatians. They were hard workers, doing a lot to impress God and others. However, Paul was grieved by them because even though they worked hard, Christ was not being formed in them (Galatians 4:19)—they had fallen away from that aspect of God's grace.

Think of it: God lives in you. He loves to prove to you that He really is there and to prove to those around you that He really is amazing from there—*what a work!* I often don't expect God will do much with me; rather, I expect *I* have to do much with me. When that way of thinking reaches its zenith, I'm a complete wreck. The flesh and adversary have successfully conspired to draw me from the real kingdom (the one to which I belong and that is in me) into a false one...and one I do not work at all well in.

God is actually in us and would love to have us know all about it. Unfortunately, we've been kept from it.

In order to see how, think of it like this: Let's say that beginning next Monday at 7:00 a.m., the Holy Spirit will take over your life for 24 hours. He will have free rein to do with you absolutely anything and everything He sees fit—no questions asked. What would you expect your day to be like, and how would you look and act in it? What might your co-workers say of you on that day, and how would your job go? On the Sunday evening before, would you be nervous or fearful?

Speaking to a church one Sunday, I asked, "What would you think and feel if I alerted you to the fact that Jesus Himself was walking into the sanctuary right now? What would you feel? Excited and ready to be loved? (Nodding heads.) And if I told you that the Father was making His way up the aisle as we speak, would you feel much the same? (Again, nodding heads.) If I told you that the Holy Spirit was about to arrive and began to count down to His appearance ('five, four, three, two, one!'), would you feel differently?"

Their answer was a unanimous sea of nodding heads. Here are the words they used to describe their feelings regarding the Holy Spirit's appearance: *nervous, panic, fear,* and *time to leave.*

Who's Afraid of the Holy Spirit?

In our day, the Holy Spirit has become the "Scary One," sort of the loose cannon of the Trinity, the One responsible for all the fireworks in the church, making us shy and standoffish about His efforts toward us. I once called a friend and said, "While in prayer, the Holy Spirit impressed upon me that He wants to talk with you about something." When I asked him what he felt, he answered, "Oh, *terrific*. I'm in trouble."

Is the Holy Spirit really the heavy of the Trinity? After all, He is the one who does all the convicting. If that's who He is and what He does, why on earth would you want to hand over your day to Him—have you ever felt like that?

After asking a group of friends what the efforts of the Holy Spirit were in their lives, the general consensus was that He revealed right from wrong for them and convicted them of sin, leading them to confession when needed. Also, He kept them in right relationship with the Father. *Not bad.* Except that was the ministry of the law under the former covenant.

At one time, believers had stone tablets and the teachings of the scribes and Pharisees to keep them in line, but now we have a very active (and capable!) Holy Spirit to do the same thing. *That's it?* Well, there's more, they said—He gives us special insight, deeper understanding, and gifts to do well in the church—you know, good stuff. All true. But not nearly enough—just pieces of the whole.

Under the old covenant, God's relationship with believing man was through a governing ministry of rules and regulations, rights and wrongs, and do's and don'ts. No one did particularly well with it, but the covenant brought something essential: awareness of sin and condemnation (Romans 3:20; 5:16) and death (7:10,13). It brought *failure* into the light and gave no assistance. Old covenant believers were forgiven. Yes, their sins were covered over by the blood of regular sacrifices, but they were continually reminded of them, sin having not yet been dealt with (Hebrews 10:3).

So is that the primary ministry of the Spirit today, to remind us of our sins so we can be forgiven through the blood of Christ? How is that any better? What's so new about that?

The Spirit Brings Out God's Successes

Riding bikes with my daughters to school brings us by the ever-vigilant crossing guard. She had a whistle in her mouth and hands at the ready to stop us or correct our direction. If we go by the rules, she smiles, and all is well. But if we do the wrong thing, she frowns, loads up her lungs, draws up her hands, and lets us have it. Is *that* a picture of the Holy Spirit's work in our lives? I'm overdoing it, I know. But, really, what's the deal?

The ministry of the law, which rightly condemned me, brought out *my failures*, but the ministry of the Spirit brings out *His success*. Read that again.

The good work of the law was always to condemn and bring death. The work of the Holy Spirit is always to rightly convince believers of our complete and eternal righteousness in Christ. One good work (that former work) brought imprisonment. The old-covenant believers were never free nor far from their sin, but through endless, repetitive sacrifices, they were ever reminded of it. (Please read Hebrews 10.) But *this* good work—*this* ministry—convinces us (or convicts us, if you like) that we have been made free from our sin through one final sacrifice and have been given the righteousness of Another, our Savior Jesus Christ! Now that's a ministry!

Read what the apostle Paul wrote, rather well acquainted himself with the two agreements God made for believers:

> He has made us competent as ministers of *a new covenant*—not of the letter but of the Spirit; for the letter kills, but the Spirit gives life. Now if the ministry that brought death, which was engraved in letters on stone, came with glory, so that the Israelites could not look steadily at the face of Moses because of its glory, fading though it was, will not the ministry of the Spirit be even more glorious? *If the ministry that condemns men is glorious, how much more glorious is the ministry that brings righteousness!* For what was glorious has no glory now in comparison with

the surpassing glory. And if what was fading away came with glory, how much greater is the glory of that which lasts! (2 Corinthians 3:6-11).

So, what are you feeling right now? Stop and think. Stop. Think.

According to the Scriptures, He is right now working to convince you of what Jesus has given you and made you to be—righteous! The biblical phrase *to convict* means to "convince utterly." What a good thing that is. However, the Holy Spirit's conviction has taken on an almost entirely negative connotation in the church today. Many Christians believe that the Spirit's conviction is a rough and dark thing, as if He were working them over or throwing them into the heavenly jail cell until they relent and agree that they are miserable, no-good wretches. "All right, Holy Spirit—you win! I'm bad. Really bad." Scripture says that "there is now no condemnation for those who are in Christ Jesus" (Romans 8:1), but we've somehow been convinced that the Spirit's work with us is the exception—as if it's okay for Him to condemn us! So it's not surprising that many of us get skittish around Him. We have even begun supposed copycat efforts of convicting ourselves.

How much of your life have you spent wondering and worrying about your right doing and wrongdoing, and how has it turned out? Have you felt the gift of God's freedom because of it, or has it removed fear or dread? Has it ever, *ever* produced the real righteous behavior of Jesus, who is your life? No.

Let the Spirit Be Your Guide

I'm not saying you should give yourself a pass on lousy, sinful behavior. Neither am I saying that God doesn't care about it anymore. That's not true. But what I am saying is that the way to good behavior is through believing in what the Spirit is saying to you, and it's far better than you suspect!

As long as behavior is your focus, a standard of behavior has your attention and gets your motivation. That combo means your failure and condemnation—mark it down. And the Spirit's ministry to you will be to no avail because you'll believe He's entirely focused on your behavior too. He isn't. It's a bad rap. Instead, He's looking at the behavior of Christ, and He knows you're in Him, in His behavior, in His history, and in His future!

And that makes something vital happen, something you may have been missing—it makes you delightfully *free.* "Where the Spirit of the Lord is, *there is freedom*" (2 Corinthians 3:17).

If, in fact, Jesus set us free *so we would be and remain free* (see Galatians 5:1), then would it surprise you that it is now the ministry of the Spirit to remind you of that freedom—how good it is, how you got it, and what it entails? He isn't convicting you so you'll hang your head and begin to engage in some anguished prayer of self-punishment or sorrowful sin offering. He already has the sin offering of Another! Yours isn't needed. In fact, it's an affront to His. Trusting in Jesus (in what He did concerning sin) is how you and I live by faith. And that's the way to live.

The chief effort of the devil, your cunning adversary, is and will be to disable the majesty of God's grace and gift to you. He cannot prevent your receiving it, but he will attempt to make it go unnoticed by you—and therefore ineffective.

But thank God that the Holy Spirit is the One who clues you in as to who you are, upon whom you rely, how much you are loved, and how to live by faith. And He's the One who gives you power to do all of that. But if we believe He is all about something else—something less—we may avoid Him and attempt to go it alone. That's when ugly and old fleshly behaviors are seemingly resurrected and begin to plague us once again, no matter how hard we try to work against them.

Real Sanctification

When I'm delighting in the incredible grace of God to me in Christ, and when I reflect on how great this new covenant made by the Father with Christ is, the fruit of the Spirit is quickly in abundance—and I'm not even working at it. Believing in Him in me, I am free to be who I am in reality, at the deepest point. I still get surprised by how great that real me is, the me in Christ, the one now sharing His nature, having been born entirely new through the work of the Spirit. In Him, I'm godly and free! And so are you.

Sanctification is simply this: By believing in who Christ is for us, we offer ourselves to the Spirit throughout the day, and His life and provision become increasingly apparent as the days progress. Isn't that what you want?

And what is His intention? In addition to being on display in a holy vessel of His choosing and making, the Spirit intends that you and I should share in the very glory of God, now in us. Now—not just later.

> But we ought always to thank God for you, brothers loved by the Lord, because from the beginning God chose you to be saved through the sanctifying work of the Spirit and through belief in the truth. He called you to this through our gospel, *that you might share in the glory of our Lord Jesus Christ* (2 Thessalonians 2:13-14).

Wow. What a plan. Have the odds of offering yourself to Him gone up? He's great to have around, great to have within, great to know! He's not the heavy you may have thought He was.

My hope—my prayer—is that you too will enjoy a fresh breeze of awareness and subsequent confidence in the Spirit now in you. Feeling condemned? It's not from Him. Feeling separated from Him? It's not true. Feeling particularly filthy today? That's not true either. Your flesh, despicable as ever, may have led you down the sad trail of temptation, there to make you stumble and to torment you, even holding out the evidence in support of the charges of the Accuser.

But the *real you*, the you God made at new birth, remains intact, unaltered, and radiant in the radiance of Another, waiting to be stimulated through the sanctifying, convincing work of the Holy Spirit.

So…feeling convicted? Me too. Isn't it great?

Questions for Discussion

1. Describe some of your thoughts and feelings about the Holy Spirit up until now.

2. Does offering yourself to Him make you nervous? Why or why not?

3. What does "to convict" mean in relation to the Holy Spirit?

4. How has your perception of the Spirit's work changed after reading this chapter?

Chapter Seven

Hitting My Pause Button

How to Find God by an Intentional Delay

Since we live by the Spirit, let us keep in step with the Spirit. Let us not become conceited, provoking and envying each other.

GALATIANS 5:25-26

There are times when even the best manager is like the little boy with the big dog, waiting to see where the dog wants to go so he can take him there.

LEE IACOCCA

Many years ago, a friend and I were trying to impress the same girl. We were each about 13 and were making awkward attempts at figuring out how to get what we wanted in life. My competition thought he could out-clever me, but she laughed a lot more following my comments than his. I won. Of course, he proceeded to beat me up. Oops. I hadn't counted on that, but that's life. Since we all lived on the same street, they could see me cower all the way home.

For years I learned to live as best I could around that guy—*way around.* For the most part, we were civil to each other, but whenever my bully was near, I could feel myself shrinking inside. I hated that feeling. I did my best to deal with it by looking confident and assured on the outside while making my way in the opposite direction.

At a large reunion party some 15 years later, a group of us were discussing what we were doing with our lives when we were joined by my bully. Around the group we went, and as doctor this, accountant that, salesperson this, and manager that elaborated on how we were doing with our dreams, it came to me.

When I said, "I'm a youth pastor," my bully scowled and asked, "Is that it?" And I felt that old shrink all over again. He'd won. After that, I wasn't the same at the party. On the two-hour drive home, I lamented to God that I felt ashamed of my title and life. Well, God loves me and thinks highly of me, and He calmed and soothed me all the way home, securing me—it turned out to be a great drive.

I had to return to that same town the very next night. Pulling into one of a hundred gas stations, I parked next to the pump and noticed my bully pulling in right next to me. *Dear God*, I thought. He got out and asked the strangest question: "Hey, Ralph! What's with all this Christian stuff, anyway?"

My first thought was, *It's my time for revenge!* I began to beat him with the gospel. Speaking in clear terms so he wouldn't miss his beating, I took him on a tour of the gospel only so I could tell him where he was sure to go. As the heat got hotter and my old resentment made me feel like Mike Tyson, in my mind I was suddenly interrupted by a question from the Holy Spirit: *You don't like him, do you?* Suddenly staring into space, I paused and was momentarily silenced. Finally I thought in response, *No. Not at all.* And the Spirit said, *But I do. Would you like My love for him?* Somehow I responded, *Yes.*

Immediately everything within me changed—I loved my bully! I found not one fault with him and had not one bit of resentment because I was so filled with love. My eyes spilling over with tears, I said, "I am a Christian because I know for sure that Jesus loves me, and that has changed everything. I cannot live without Him. He loves you amazingly and longs to show you what He is like toward you. His love for you is intense, and when you are ready to ask Him to show you what He is like toward you, He will. You've only to ask."

With his head cocked to one side and his eyes and mouth wide open, my bully stammered, "Uh, I've never heard anything like that in my life. Thank you. Thank you."

That night at the gas station, I felt and knew the love of God for someone I thought I despised. There had been no strategy for it, no working it up, and no earning it. But the One who lives in me had something in mind, and He convinced me to say yes to His love. Frankly, the last thing I wanted was love for my bully, and it was probably the last thing he wanted—neither of us liked each other! Yet God in me produced what He thought and felt, and I was deeply involved. Oddly, it felt like me too.

That was several years ago, and even though I haven't seen my bully since, the pursuit of my life has never been the same. (About a year ago I learned that my bully, after making a notable mess of things, had become a Christian and had begun a ministry to inner-city youth. I guess God really does love him!) From that day to this, my primary passion has been to know Christ in me in such a way that He might live evidently through me. That one desire has provided the direction for my life, moving me from place to place, from singleness to marriage, and from ministry to ministry.

In order to find Him in me, two things that we looked at in the last chapter had to happen. First, I had to believe He was there. Second, I had to look for Him. And now I would add a third aspect: *I have to momentarily do nothing.* And that's not easy.

Lazarus

When Jesus walked among us, sickness was at least as frightening as it is today and usually quicker to cause death. Remember the men who dug through a roof, lowering their sick friend into the house below so Jesus could heal him (Mark 2:1-12; Luke 5:17-26)? If you or someone you loved were sick, and you knew a way back to health, you wouldn't hesitate to take advantage. So it shouldn't be surprising that people who knew Jesus would clamor for His attention concerning a sick relative.

We find another such situation in the book of John:

> Now a man named Lazarus was sick. He was from Beth-
> any, the village of Mary and her sister Martha. This Mary,
> whose brother Lazarus now lay sick, was the same one
> who poured perfume on the Lord and wiped his feet with

her hair. So the sisters sent word to Jesus, "Lord, the one you love is sick." When he heard this, Jesus said, "This sickness will not end in death. No, it is for God's glory so that God's Son may be glorified through it." Jesus loved Martha and her sister and Lazarus. Yet when he heard that Lazarus was sick, he stayed where he was two more days (John 11:1-6).

What did Jesus do when the sisters presented their concern to Him? What were His actions toward those He loved? He did nothing! In fact, Jesus remained where He was for a couple more days. Why?

Even as Jesus lived fully as a human being, He lived every day and every moment fully dependent upon the Father for direction and provision (see John 5:19,30). He didn't do a thing without Him. And so, no matter how briefly, *Jesus paused.* And in that moment of delay, the Father communicated with the Son that He should do nothing because the Father had something planned to demonstrate His own glory. This sickness wasn't the earthly end for Lazarus. (To see how the rest of the story came out, read John 11:7-44.)

Jesus' pause (His momentary "do-nothing") was a pause of faith, and that's why He knew to do nothing after it. He believed the Father would speak to Him because the Father had a supreme interest in the situation, and Jesus believed He would hear Him. In faith, Jesus spoke to the sisters' messenger and, free from the demanding urgency of the moment, got on with the next issue at hand.

If I had been there, I might have thought, *What! How can You have no concern? How can You not do something—and these are Your friends! And look around! Everyone's watching! What a perfect time to do something for the glory of God! And You do nothing? I can't believe it!*

Your Personal Pause Button

Jesus *was* doing something for the glory of God, and we would do well to live after the same manner as He did. As Jesus did, hitting our personal pause button in the face of urgent needs and desires means we believe *something else defines reality* and that *Someone else* may well have something He'd like to do. That's faith! While it can be very difficult in the face of pressing needs and desires, pausing on purpose is one of the most significant points of faith I know. If you believe that God lives in you, knows everything—*everything*— and that He can do something about everything, why not take a moment, a fraction of a second, to look and listen for Him? This is how to get a healthy and godly perceiver-expresser!

A faith-filled delay is a terrific blow against the devil and the flesh because they would love to circumnavigate God in you by seducing you to do something *reasonable* or *responsible* in the press of the moment. The flesh would have you do anything—*anything*—but pause on purpose, listening for the Holy Spirit who lives in you. Think of the threat *that* is to all things demonic! By a simple delay, we can know God and follow His leading, whether that's to say something, say nothing, do something, do nothing, or simply hear Him or share in His feelings. When we wait expectantly for Him, we, who are so often transfixed and motivated by all things temporal and visible, bring great glory and honor "to the King *eternal*, immortal, *invisible*" (1 Timothy 1:17). This is how to know what's *really* going on in light of present circumstances. This is how to be free of the temporal demand (when we think we need to quickly do something) because we're sowing toward eternity! If God knows what will happen before it happens, why not seek His counsel? Here's why: We've been taking another route.

The Superiority of Christ

As we saw in chapter 4, the flesh has long offered us a way to get through life, to get what we need, to look good in front of others, and to avoid what we don't want. For most, it has become normal— living by the flesh is how we live. But Paul wrote of a normal way to live for those born of the Spirit—the highest way: "I consider everything a loss compared to the surpassing greatness of *knowing Christ Jesus* my Lord, for whose sake I have lost all things. I consider them rubbish, that I may gain Christ" (Philippians 3:8).

Wow! He really meant it. That's what happens when we resist the press of the moment and don't try to give an answer that makes us look good or come up with something clever or cute. Instead, we momentarily do nothing—we pause with an inner question: *What are Your thoughts, Jesus? What do You feel about this? Is there something You would like to do? I have faith in You, my Lord.*

If our highest goal is to know God right in front of people and situations, we will resist the urge of the flesh. If it isn't, and if we don't look toward the invisible world, most of our efforts will go toward adjusting to this visible world, to make it a better place, to get along comfortably within it, to keep ourselves as happy and fulfilled as we can, and to assist others toward the same ends by the same means. And yet, from God's perspective we may be failing, unintentionally living by the influence of the flesh—living without the life of God.

Why would Christians live under the influence of the flesh? The answer is that they don't believe in the incredible extent of God's grace to us in Christ, and so they live in order to get and manage life by other means.

That's no crime, and we're not stupid. Most of our life has sent us the message that God is unreliable concerning our needs and desires, so we'd better control them. If you want to avoid rejection, do this. If you want to steer clear of failure, do that. If you want to be popular, do this. If you want to get ahead, do that. *Control yourself*, and you will *control life.*

That's the bait. Swallow it and you'll learn to live to have control rather than live to have Him.

The problem we're having is that we're confusing the life we can have with the life God produces, and the two are different. One kind of life is our life*style*. We have it by choosing the right techniques, living by the right principles, and by offering ourselves to the best efforts. *Control yourself* and you will control life. The other kind of life is the life that moves us from the inside toward the outside. It can be found by believing and offering yourself to the Holy Spirit, who will produce in you what God is like.

But if we don't do that, we will live in order to find the just-right prescription of how to win at life. That will always result in failure and frustration for the sons and daughters of God. They will have exchanged knowing God for having their own control. Is that what we want? Life by the Spirit exchanged for life by the flesh? Fortunately, believers living by the flesh will eventually feel uncomfortable, unnatural, and out of step with the Spirit because they've been taken hostage to something not at all like them.

Avenues of the Flesh

How did the flesh entrap us? We know that throughout our lives, external forces have induced us to believe the lie that God is not capable or reliable to help us; therefore, we chose the avenue offered by the flesh. You and I will know that avenue as something that feels relatively secure (a way to get what we want or avoid what we don't want), but it will be flesh, all the same.

To help you see the avenues of your flesh, I've made up some names for those common ways of living to control life that unintentionally sacrifice both knowing God and *life* from God. See if you recognize how the flesh has led you away from knowing God by offering you control. Keep in mind that this fleshly activity is not you, but something which influences and drives you—you don't want it anymore.

Chicken Flesh

In most every conflict, you quickly feel like running away—like getting out of there. Life as you like it feels threatened, and the best course of action is to leave. If you must remain, you'd better walk on eggshells because you just don't know what might happen. Go chicken and run. I have this flesh. Now, sometimes you *should* leave, especially if you truly are at risk. But this flesh suggests an exodus course for life whenever a decent argument or stressful circumstance occurs. Pausing to listen to the Spirit isn't on the menu at all. But it could be.

After returning from a long day of substitute teaching, my wife,

Sarah, was particularly annoyed—I could feel it. No longer was she bothered only by unruly kids. She was bothered by traffic on the way home, by unhelpful teaching assistants, by ill-fitting clothing, and by the weather. Feeling her irritation, this thought presented itself to me: *Don't say anything. Just quietly walk away and let her blow off steam. You know how she gets. This tension in the room is a bad feeling, isn't it? Walk away, and you will feel better.* Frankly, Sarah doesn't lash out at me, she doesn't take it out on me, and I'm not at all at risk. But in the conflict, my flesh offers me a way of living that will eventually allow the flesh to behave through me. In the short run, it feels like I escape. In the long run, I take a beating when the flesh, having successfully led me away from the Spirit, behaves through me.

Well, that day, while feeling every bit of the conflict, *I paused* and offered myself to the Spirit. Immediately I heard the Spirit say, "You are well. Go and rescue your wife." Feeling better but hearing nothing more, I approached Sarah and said, "I love you." Remaining open to the Spirit, confident He would shape my words, I continued by saying, "You have been roughed up today by the world, which can never accurately identify you. Always it will resist who you are in Christ, never reflecting back the honor and glory due you. If you're tired and worn out, it's not because you have failed. It's because you've been in a struggle with a worldly system that makes little room for you. According to God, you're the best there is in this world, even as it rejects you. You're wonderful."

She was immediately revived. By my act of sowing to the Holy Spirit, He produced in me *faithfulness, self-control, peace, gentleness,* and *love.* Holding one another, we knew who we were—the sacred children of God. And we loved! And we had *life.*

Brute Flesh

This fleshly driven person gets along in life by snuffing out disagreements and abruptly ending dialogue with, "I don't want to hear it anymore! That's it! We're done!" Leaning toward the other party with eyes narrowed and fists clenched, brute flesh demands, "Got it? Are we clear?" which means, "It's my way or the highway—you choose!" This believer has learned to rule the roost by inducing fear in those around him. He walks around with an invisible line drawn in the sand. Cross him, and he will cross you. Everyone knows Mr. Brute is not to be messed with because what he gives in return is way too dangerous. To be clear, this fleshly led person doesn't just rarely lose it and brute his way to a conclusion he wants—he does it regularly, for it has become a way of navigating life. It isn't him, but he doesn't know it, having found no better way to live. But there is a better way, and a pause will help him find it.

NASCAR Flesh

What works for this fleshly driven Christian is life at 160 miles per hour. Pit stops are very rare, and even then, work is part of lunch, business part of breakfast, and strategy a part of most every relationship. A key sign that NASCAR flesh is in operation is that this person feels truly guilty when sickness lays him out, incapacitating him. Waiting upon the Holy Spirit and sowing toward Him doesn't fit with the need for speed that drives this fleshly believer. Resting in Christ is a foreign language to him. You can help him, not by telling him to slow down or by waving him into the pits (he's liable to run you over!), but by asking him questions: What do you think God's opinion is on this matter? What are God's feelings for you right now? If he cannot answer (he's going 160), the Holy Spirit will later bring to his mind the questions you've posted there.

Unfortunately, because these people get a lot done, they rarely look for help from God. Instead, they burn out. The way to wellness is not to manage themselves better (they'll do it as fast as they can) but to believe God lives in them and wants to provide from there. Only that pleasure will induce this driven believer to slow down.

Nike Flesh

"Just do it" is this person's motto. "Git 'er done" comes in a close second. While speed is not their issue, task accomplishment is—they live for it, and that's the problem. They have allowed measurable accomplishment to take the place of knowing God. They only feel better when their tasks are completed to their satisfaction, and nothing brings them more peace than that. Their prayer life is overwhelmingly themed with sincere requests about what to do. The flesh has sown a lie to them that God is to be known because He is useful. He always has a plan to make life work. If they can get to Him, He is sure to tell them what it is, and that's what's most important. But it isn't.

These believers are often employed as administrators and project managers—they're terrific at getting jobs done. They're not so terrific at relaxing with people. They'll fidget and wonder what tasks could be getting done instead…and drift away to do them. Instead of commanding them—"Sit down and spend some time with me, Martha!"—you can help them by sowing to the Spirit and perhaps asking a question or two: What do you think God is thinking right now? If He were to suddenly show up, what would He want for you? They may initially feel uncomfortable with your questions, but when they know you're not trying to corral and break them but instead usher them toward life by the Spirit, they will begin to pay attention. Remember, Nike flesh people are God's project—not ours.

Cavalry Flesh

These believers are driven away from knowing and relying upon the Holy Spirit in them by the lure to rescue. They live by the trumpet call of the cavalry and always have a fast horse waiting. Every need they hear about beckons them to devise a way to bring comfort quickly. Any emotional pain or unresolved relational mess launches them toward resolution. They must help you be well because wellness is everything! After all, isn't God the Great Physician? Unfortunately, they can interrupt a work of the Spirit, who has something deeper and more lasting in mind than a simple surface healing. For those with Cavalry flesh, sanctification is less about being genuinely transformed in cooperation with the Holy Spirit, and it is more about feeling better about oneself. When these habit-formed

Christians hear the trumpet call of need, they must resist the fleshly demand by pausing and offering themselves to the Spirit. Their thrill in life will be found in knowing Him who is, indeed, the Rescuer. They will love being included in the big picture of His rescue and will learn to relax in light of His plan and ability.

Sunny-day Flesh

If you're driven by the belief that life is good only when everything is positive, you may have sunny-day flesh. Frankly, everything in my life isn't good, everything isn't positive, and I'm not always encouraged—these are facts, and they're okay! They're normal. However, believers driven by this flesh have always got to put a positive spin on everything. It's how they've learned to live. These are good yet fleshly people to visit (they're your cheerleaders!), but they're no fun to live with because they'll attempt to orchestrate you to be good and happy at all times too. If you're having a marginally bad moment and would like to know Jesus in it, they will overwhelm you with optimism, driving you up and out of your downer day. They must have everything and everyone just right in order to move ahead and live— that's the lie. Even though Jesus said that, like Him, we would be well acquainted with suffering, there is little place for that for those with this type of flesh.

So when trial or difficulty is presented to them, they manage life by staying upbeat and positive, not by pausing and turning toward the Holy Spirit, who has much to say and do for them. See the twist? Nothing is wrong with being positive unless it becomes a manner of life, keeping you from knowing the life of God within. With help, these believers will have the load of the world taken from their shoulders (after all, they've been responsible to make it happy) and will find the joy of Christ produced in them. You want to be around them when that happens because it is a delight to behold.

IRYW Flesh

This brand of flesh ("I'm Right, You're Wrong") contends that being right is everything—the supreme motivation. They read their Bibles not so much to know the One it speaks about, but to be right in doctrine, correct in discussion, and free from wrong, the scary opposite of right. When an opinionated discussion blows in, they navigate it with, "Yeah, but…" and "Well, but…" and even "True, but…" all to show that they are more right than others are. The way to help them is not to show them they're wrong (though you may be tempted), but to not play the argumentative game at all. When they see how this fleshly lure affects them, given that they're often identified as arrogant and prideful, they may see that their flesh is keeping them from the delight of the Holy Spirit. Then they will quiet down and not have to end every conversation with a victory. Instead, they will be knowing the One who really is always right, and that will be sufficient and satisfying. With an intentional pause, He will provide for them what their flesh has been seductively offering: peace, comfort, and security.

Whiny Flesh

To some of us, life has sent the message that if we whine and whimper, we get what we want. Whine and we get fed. Whimper and we don't get punished. Whine and we get noticed. Whimper and we get sympathy. If this fleshly course of action has succeeded for long, evidence of its effectiveness makes it a challenge to take another course of action. When a whine works, pausing instead to think of the Spirit seems ineffective. And it is—if getting what we want is more important to us than knowing God! That's the trick. Smacking a "No whiners allowed!" sticker on their forehead doesn't work; it will only frustrate them because it does nothing toward the Spirit, who is having the conflict within.

Rather than interpret lots of situations as worthy of a whine, these fleshly Christians need to see the conflict within for what it is. "I want something, and I'm afraid God won't give it to me—He is insufficient here. So, this is an alternate course to get what I want." When they see how ugly that belief is, they will likely begin turning away from the avenue of the flesh toward the Holy Spirit…and that whine you've been hearing will stop.

Detective Flesh

These flesh-driven people come at you with all the warmth of a microscope. They over-examine most everything, including you and everything you say—they make you uncomfortable. It's not so much that they want to get to know you as it is that they want to find something, something they suspect you're hiding. They think everyone is an unsolved mystery with dangerous twists and turns and hidden secrets, which, if revealed, might shock the world. In fact, they think everyone is *their* mystery to solve. So they dig for clues.

Detective-flesh people will ask probing questions and then draw conclusions about you, sometimes right in front of you, as if you were no longer there. "So, then, Ralph's a twin and a middle child, which means he's a peace-loving negotiator, doesn't like strife, and wants to be liked. Most likely a sanguine too; so he loves a crowd… Hmm."

Through the years of their experience, they have come to believe that knowing as much as they can about everyone and everything will keep them safe. Knowledge means control, and that's a powerful motivator. They want to know every angle on everyone that could possibly hurt or disappoint them—make sure everything is out of everyone's closet. They'll drag it out if they need to. Frankly, they may have good reason, having been surprised and wounded in the past. You shouldn't be quick to blame them (or others) for falling to a seemingly advantageous way of life offered by the flesh. They dislike the unknown because it may hurt them. Often these believers will be at least somewhat correct in their assessment of people, and that can be valuable.

But they're trapped—bound to make assessments and careful to keep people away from their hearts. Detective-flesh people seal off their hearts as though dealing with a crime scene—wearing gloves and masking their faces when interacting with others. They may touch you, but they won't get close. They won't remove their protective coverings unless they find something better fitting—the safety of the Holy Spirit, who knows everything about everyone already. He is certain to alert them and clue them in when needed. In Him, they will have what they have been seeking—*security.*

The List Goes On

Frankly, there are many more:

- *Martyr flesh.* "If I don't do it, nobody will!" motivates these fleshly believers' resentment-filled days.

- *Octopus flesh.* These Christians look for the angle that gives them the advantage in everything.

- *Scrooge flesh.* You can figure that one out.

- *Magnifier flesh.* Everything is made out to be worse than it actually is.

- *Fixer-upper flesh.* Nearly everyone they meet begs the just-right touch that will make them just right for the marketplace.

- *Loner flesh.* These people believe and act on the lie that there's no place in the body of Christ for them.

- *Barbie flesh.* Unless they look their best at all times, something tragic will happen. For them, life is a parade.

- *Linear flesh.* Life is just waiting for them to finally get it right, and when they do, *then* they will really be living. They may not know God, but they'll be living.

And on and on it goes.

When I bring some of these fleshly lures to light at seminars, invariably the audience begins to see how their particular flesh has kept them from sowing to the Spirit by offering another way, and they've seen the results. They haven't found God particularly satisfying or capable. When they begin making up their own labels for the flesh, I know they've got it. The secret lure away from the Holy Spirit has been revealed as worthless tin.

I should hasten to add that some of these characteristics can be a part of our natural, God-given personality. Some of us are simply wired by God to notice people. And sometimes you just have to do or say something immediately, wondering later if what you did or said was by the Spirit. Sometimes that's simply the way it is, and it's okay. God works in us that way too. (And remember, this isn't a way for you to *finally* do things *just right* with God—at last earning His elusive approval. It is another way to know and enjoy Him, and He'll be glorified in that.) It's just that most of the time, we're not waiting at all, but rushing into the conflict and into the scene too soon—wanting and working to get something done. That's the lure, and we miss the Holy Spirit because we're after the fleshly bait.

So What Do We Do?

Doing absolutely nothing is not the solution; neither is ignoring the lure. Offering yourself to the Spirit when the lure drags by your face is the course you want because life is with Him. It is a new way to live, to be sure, and growing into it most likely won't happen by this time tomorrow. But over time, it will happen because it is *the* way—He will bring you to it: "But now, by dying to what once bound us, we have been released from the law so that we serve in the new way of the Spirit, and not in the old way of the written code" (Romans 7:6).

It should be evident that those of us under the influence of the flesh may look particularly bad, or we may look particularly *good*. And that's a more difficult thing to see and a more difficult thing from which to turn. But it's just as fleshly, just as foreign, and just as dangerous. I might appear to be the most faithful church attender in the world, but I might be doing it because I fear God will bless me *only if I do* and not at all if I don't. So I go…under the influence. I don't mean to imply that regular church attendance is a bad thing. It isn't. It's just that under the influence of the flesh, it becomes *the thing*. Going to church gets the greater emphasis—not knowing God. The evidence might include condemning thoughts and feelings toward those who fail to attend as regularly. Or I might frequently and strongly encourage others to attend as the solution to their lack of blessing or, perhaps, I take a leadership position on the let's-get-the-church-to-church-on-time-every-Sunday committee. I'm active but nevertheless fleshly.

Under this influence, I'm not free to ask and trace out the godly and good reasons for going to a gathering, sowing to the Spirit and following His leading, finding His gifts in me to do this or that, and living by faith. Instead, I'm captive to what looks right and to what ought to be, and that's where the flesh is found.

Fleshly activity is not you but something that influences and drives you—it should be much more evident having read this chapter. Should we now run off and point out each other's flesh types? Be very careful because the flesh—and not the Spirit—may be motivating you to do that. It's not hard to imagine the fun you could have with this new knowledge. That could become as fleshly a lure as anything else. Resist the nibble by pausing to offer yourself to the Holy Spirit. "Since we live by the Spirit, let us keep in step with the Spirit. Let us not become conceited, provoking and envying each other" (Galatians 5:25-26).

The flesh is not you, but it would like to provide a way for you to look. If you follow its tin lure of promised control, it will behave through you. You know how that will look and feel, and you want to be done with it. Now that you know better, now that you believe life by the Spirit is both possible and desirable, chances are good you'll refuse the bait and go for the Spirit. All it takes is an expectant pause.

And that's good news.

Questions for Discussion

1. Why is a momentary "do-nothing" an act of faith in God?

2. Why has it been tempting for you to live under the influence of the flesh?

3. What are some names or ways of describing your flesh?

4. Why is fleshly activity *not you*?

Chapter Eight

Doin' the Monster Mash

Slaying the Sin-loving Beast in You

Does God give you his Spirit and work miracles
among you because you observe the law, or
because you believe what you heard?

GALATIANS 3:5

Always go to other people's funerals, otherwise
they won't come to yours.

YOGI BERRA

About a dozen of us from my church were squirming uncomfort-
ably in our seats. As we gathered together with hundreds of
others for a men's retreat at a Christian camp, the speaker was really
giving it to us. We felt as though we deserved it.

"Do you pray every day with your wife? Do you? Why not? Don't
you know you're inviting the legions of hell into your house? There
is no excuse, especially when so much is at stake! You must pray
with your wife every day! Every day! *Ehhhhhhhvvvrrreeeeeeee* day!
Until you do, you can't expect God to honor you! You must commit to it! Before the Lord, you must commit to praying with your
wife every day!"

A week or two later, I took an informal poll. When I asked how
their prayer commitment was going, every head dropped. Though
all of us agreed with the speaker that we should pray every day with
our wives, none of us had followed through.

"I meant to," one said, "I even put it in my Day-Timer. But it just
didn't seem to work out."

Another said, "I've been feeling guilty ever since." (Nods from all the men.) "I guess I'm just not a prayer warrior…Seems like it has affected all of my prayer life."

One more said, "I thought I could do it—I've wanted to! But it seems like the way I once was before I accepted Jesus gets back into the picture and messes me up. I thought all that was buried and gone."

We were not a happy bunch.

Behaving Like the Old "I"

Do you ever behave in the poor way you did before you became a Christian? Do you ever struggle with the same temptations you did before your new life in Christ? No matter how much you pray and fight against them, do some of those old ugly desires and thoughts rise from the dead and put you to shame?

Me too.

If that old nasty "I" was crucified with Christ, what beckons to the seeming graveyard of my life, inducing the monster in me to rise from the dead? What is it that so stimulates the flesh that I cannot resist its bidding?

I remember as a small boy dancing to Bobby Pickett's classic, "The Monster Mash." It wasn't well choreographed, but it sure was fun, and I've danced to it nearly every October since. In the song, a jolt of electricity got the otherwise dead monsters "mashing" and doing what monsters do—acting monstrously. What would you expect of a monster? Without the electrical stimulus, the monsters were powerless.

But what is it that gets the monster in me going? What's the terrible power that arouses my fleshly monster toward sin? Rules. Pledges. Should-don'ts. Should-do's. Laws.

If you want to see your monster mash (the flesh in you), and if you want to stimulate inner turmoil, try living by rules for behavior, or try defining the success of your life by making pledges you must keep. Try living by law. Stimulated, the awful desires of the flesh will rise up and put you down, connecting with your perceiver-expresser. And the monster will be doin' the mash in and through you.

This is what Paul had to say about living by the law:

> Do you not know, brothers—for I am speaking to men who know the law—that the law has authority over a man only as long as he lives? For example, by law a married woman is bound to her husband as long as he is alive, but if her husband dies, she is released from the law of marriage. So then, if she marries another man while her husband is still alive, she is called an adulteress. But if her husband dies, she is released from that law and is not an adulteress, even though she marries another man. So, my brothers, you also died to the law through the body of Christ, that you might belong to another, to him who was raised from the dead, in order that we might bear fruit to God. For when we were controlled by the sinful nature [flesh], *the sinful passions aroused by the law* were at work in our bodies, so that we bore fruit for death. But now, by dying to what once bound us, we have been released from the law so that we serve in the new way of the Spirit, and not in the old way of the written code (Romans 7:1-6).

The main point is that, since we've died to the law through the body of Christ (we were crucified with Him), we are now to live and serve by the Spirit, not by the law. It's a completely new way for a completely new you.

Yet if we attempt to live by the "old way of the written code," focusing upon commandments for behavior in order to secure God's favor or to improve our life, we get all fouled up. Look at Romans 7:5. What is it that arouses sinful desires? What makes your monster mash your life? Rules. Laws. Pledges.

Do you see it?

Don't Break This Law

Try this: Do not think about a pink elephant. Don't do it. Do not imagine a long, pinkish trunk with two little hairy holes at the end. And do not think about its enormous ears, nor the two long, white things protruding from its mouth. What are those called? Oh, yeah, tusks. Don't think about them either.

Well, how did you do? Were you even a little successful? During a recent seminar, I proposed the same assignment to a willing volunteer who informed us that he had done pretty well. "I thought about a car instead," he said, "and got, oh, about a 65 percent." Someone in the room blurted, "But that means *you failed*! And I watched your face— you were all tight and forcing yourself not to think about the pink elephant, which means you were still thinking about it!" And so he was.

You know how it is with the law—you break one just a little, and you've broken it completely.

Telling someone what not to do (don't think of a hot fudge sundae) is a simple example (with nuts on top) that shows you the power of rules (and whipping cream and a cherry) to stimulate failure. Works every time! It's supposed to—God designed it that way. He didn't give the law to civilize men or to make society function nicely. "The law was added *so that* the trespass might increase" (Romans 5:20). That was the plan.

Want to watch someone's trespasses increase? On a Friday night, load 'em up with a bunch of laws—righteous should-do's and should-don'ts for the weekend—and then bid them a fond farewell. You've ruined their weekend. No matter how many of your targeted dos and don'ts they hit, they won't hit them all, and they'll be fairly miserable because of it. Even at 95 percent, they will have failed.

No one knows just what sin is until a target is put up. The moment you hear, "Don't do this, and don't do that," a very old curse (Galatians 3:10) comes immediately into effect through the power of two laws, both of which are found in Romans 7. Paul, well acquainted with his own monster, writes, "For in my inner being I delight in *God's law*; but I see *another law* at work in the members of my body, waging war against the law of my mind and *making me a prisoner of the law of sin* at work within my members" (Romans 7:22-23).

Paul identifies himself as "a prisoner," but not as he used the word elsewhere, as in his service to Jesus (Ephesians 3:1; 4:1). He sees a bondage in himself, and he is captive to it. Now, reflect for a moment. Is a prisoner (someone behind bars) necessarily committing a crime right now? Behind bars, is he engaging in criminal activity? Probably not. Why not? Prison guards are watching and warning him all the time. Is he a changed man? Who knows? He is restrained and fearful—restrained by rules and fearful of the authorities. You really have no idea what he's actually like because, imprisoned, he's in bondage. He's toeing the line. He has to be let out in order for us to see what he's really like. There's no other way. Until then, he doesn't have much of a life.

Believers Behind Bars

This is how many believers live today—imprisoned. They are restrained by rules and are fearful of *The Authority*. Early in their beginning with the church, they began receiving the rules of the kingdom, the way things are done when you're a Christian, the behaviors and activities that will keep you in good order. As soon as you violate them or cross the line, you're going to get it. So, sit up straight, get up at 6:00 and turn the lights out at 10:00, read only approved materials, pray daily, tithe, treat others with respect, and obey the laws. "Off you go, now. There's a good Christian."

What are they really like? What would they do, how would they act if we took off their restraints? We don't know. They're captives. They're toeing the line.

This explains why when we talk with people about intimacy with God, they think of something like spending a weekend in a cabin at the lake with the prison warden! Why would they go there?

Those who attempt to please God by doing their utmost to keep His commands will be plagued by fear while restrained by rules, and they will be made prisoners—slaves to the law of sin. And in their self-imposed restraint, they will lock out the love of the One who makes men free and calls them His friend. (The New Testament makes no allowance of less obedience, but the way of obedience is less of a strict grind than it is an indulgence. More about that in chapter 13.)

It gets worse. These two laws, *God's law* and the *law of sin*, always work together to produce failure for all who attempt to live by them. Always and for all. You, me, Paul, Billy Graham, the pope—everybody. All are imprisoned by them and forced into failure.

Look again at Romans 7:5. "For while we were in the flesh, *the sinful passions, which were aroused by the Law,* were at work in the members of our body to bear fruit for death" (NASB).

What powers up our monster mash? What is it that stimulates the flesh? Rules. Must-do's. Must-don'ts. Laws arouse sin.

So think about it. How does the devil fool the believer? What's his tactic to trip up the believer, frustrate him, and get him to fail? He gets him to live by rules. The flesh or the devil will suggest something like, "You know how you've been doing lately...you've got to do better. You'd better get with it." Convinced, we nod in agreement, rededicate our lives to God, begin again to focus upon what we're supposed to do and not do, and pray prayers like this: "Lord, help me to do the things You want me to do." In other words, "Help me keep Your rules."

Turn up the music because you're about to do the monster mash— welcome to the flesh! There is nothing so effective in showing people what failure and sin is and how it works as the pronouncement of rules and laws. God intended it to be so. The apostle Paul writes, "What shall we say, then? Is the law sin? Certainly not! Indeed I would not have known what sin was *except* through the law. For I would not have known what coveting really was if the law had not said, 'Do not covet'" (Romans 7:7).

Sin Takes the Opportunity

I can tell you—it works! It's perfectly effective! Why then would we think we can now live by rules in such a way as to break the intended effect? "But sin, seizing the opportunity *afforded by the commandment,* produced in me every kind of covetous desire. For apart from law, sin is dead" (Romans 7:8). Did you get that last sentence? Turn it around and it would read, "Sin is dead without laws to invigorate it." The very power of sin is the law (see 1 Corinthians 15:56).

And we try to live by it? That's crazy. No, that's demonic.

Any approach to Christian living that focuses and depends upon keeping rules as the means of experiencing spiritual growth or victory binds you to sin because you're arousing the wrong self, the pretender self, the *monster!* Each time you tack up a new pledge of obedience on the wall of your mind, an assault has already begun. "I promise" and "I commit" are the well-intentioned responses to an invitation from the flesh to a battle that it is sure to win. That's why it is so quick and happy to respond to your promises. "Thank you, Ralph, for calling and inviting me to dance. I'll take the lead now." And here comes living without the life of God.

In chapter 5, we looked at how that dance will go with the flesh in the lead. "Sexual immorality, impurity and debauchery; idolatry and witchcraft; hatred, discord, jealousy, fits of rage, selfish ambition, dissensions, factions and envy; drunkenness, orgies, and the like" (Galatians 5:19-21). How ugly that dance makes the captured Christian look, a noble one being pushed and abused all over the dance floor of life!

Have you seen it? Have you danced the terrible dance? I have too. It helps to know *it's not your dance,* and you're not in the lead, and it will help to know how to take the lead and really live and dance the way you were redesigned. It'll be beautiful. It's your design and your destiny. "Thanks be to God! He gives us the victory through our Lord Jesus Christ" (1 Corinthians 15:57).

A New Way to Dance

There's a new way to live, a new way to dance that you'll love and that is in keeping with who and what you are. It's your new normal, the new way of the Spirit. Jesus completed and canceled the former covenant, making it obsolete and releasing us from its harsh instruction so we may live by faith in Him (see Galatians 3:23-25). Your new way to live is by the grace and leading of the Holy Spirit now in you, and while that takes some getting used to, there's nothing better!

Watchman Nee agrees:

> Grace means that God does something for me; law means that I do something for God. God has certain holy and righteous demands which He places upon me; that is law. Now if law means that God requires something of me for their fulfillment, then deliverance from law means that He no longer requires that from me, but Himself provides it. Law implies that God requires me to do something for Him; deliverance from law implies that He exempts me from doing it, and that in grace He does it Himself. I need do nothing for God: that is deliverance from law.*

You died to the laws that you might live to Jesus. Fantastic! Law-keeping might hold out the promise of godly living, and you might pull it off—for a time. But law-keeping and perfect behavior will never produce intimacy with God. Instead, it will put you back into the prison of failure and return you to a fearful relationship with God as "the warden," just like Paul. Intimacy with your loving Father will lead to His behavior coming through you, His child.

And that's the way to dance, as Paul found out:

> Therefore, there is now no condemnation for those who are in Christ Jesus, because through Christ Jesus the law of the Spirit of life set me free from the law of sin and death. For what the law was powerless to do in that it was

---

* Watchman Nee, *The Normal Christian Life* (Carol Stream, IL: Tyndale House Publishers, 1977), 156.

weakened by the sinful nature, God did by sending his own Son in the likeness of sinful man to be a sin offering. And so he condemned sin in sinful man, in order that the righteous requirements of the law might be fully met in us, who do not live according to the sinful nature [flesh] but according to the Spirit (Romans 8:1-4).

Questions for Discussion

1. What stimulates the flesh?

2. How could you really mess up a Christian friend?

3. What happens when you put *God's law* and the *law of sin* together? Have you noticed this problem in your life? How?

4. Have you gotten to know God better by commitments and rule-keeping?

Chapter Nine

Cleaning Up Toxic Relationships
Getting Free from the Prison of Devotion

But now, by dying to what once bound us, we have been
released from the law so that we serve in the new way of
the Spirit, and not in the old way of the written code.

ROMANS 7:6

I told my psychiatrist that everyone hates me. He said I
was being ridiculous—everyone hasn't met me yet.

RODNEY DANGERFIELD

If Jesus wanted to tag along and interact with everyone you know
and everyone you meet, would you be encouraged to invite Him?
Would you trust Him to talk with and treat each person just the way
He wanted? The night before your first day together, would you be
excited? What do you think your day would be like? What if you
could live like that every day, with Jesus as your tagalong? Would
you have to worry about how you would treat everyone? Would you
be concerned with whether or not your relational skills were sufficient for each relationship and every meeting?

What's to worry? You'd have Jesus with you, and however your
encounters went, people would think of you in relation to Him.
Frankly, He would soon become the headliner and you the tagalong.
You wouldn't mind, would you? It would sure mean life from a different angle, wouldn't it?

I ask all these questions because I want to get your hopes up
and prepare you for a royal burden-lifting. Because you're maturing in Christ and learning to live by the Spirit, you should expect it.

Perhaps, far back on the shelf of expectation, you've long ago left any real hope of finding rest as a direct result of your life in Christ. It's time to take up your hope, dust it off, and have a new look.

How Do You Do with Relationships?

In our day one of the biggest concerns we have is how to successfully navigate relationships. If you think of the books you've read, the sermons you've heard, the rules at work, even the classroom time devoted to how we're to treat others, you will see how deeply involved we are with relationships. Our ability is almost constantly on trial, the demand to perform is around every corner, and a report card is offered at nearly every meeting. We're focused on relationships.

So tell me, how do you do with relationships? What kind of people get under your skin, and what are you doing about that? Are you submitting to leaders from your heart? Are you treating your spouse the way you're supposed to? Do you think of yourself as too blunt or too reserved? Too shy or too outgoing? Too quick to commit or too slow? Probably you've thought of all these things because you estimate yourself by how you do with people, like the rest of us. It judges our days. Our interaction with others is the white-hot spotlight on the stage of our life, and everybody's looking. Everybody sees.

Because of this audience, the pressure to come up with the just-right performance might well be the lure that makes actors of us while robbing us of the heart for what we're doing. And it might be the single most effective lure cast through this world that draws us away from life by the Spirit and knowing Jesus throughout the day.

The Marriage Relationship

The apostle Paul has some interesting things to say about the marriage relationship. At first reading it will seem terribly irresponsible. It always does when I read it as the first Scripture to begin a Christian marriage seminar or retreat: "What I mean, brothers, is that the time is short. *From now on those who have wives should live as if they had none*" (1 Corinthians 7:29).

Silence. Every eye is on me. Immediately, I've got their attention. True, some are bothered with me and nearly all are confused, but they're listening. Most don't think it's in the Bible, but I believe it is one of the most important introductions for Christian living found in Scripture.

Got a wife? Live as though you didn't. Just get a husband? Keep living the way you were before you did. That's best. That'll work. "Got it everyone? Okay, let's go home," I joke.

"How does this square with marriage?" their faces question. "How can we live like that and have a good marriage?" Good questions—ones the Holy Spirit wanted to address to the Corinthians through Paul because something other than a good marriage was His first goal, something that would be the greatest influence for marriage and all of our relationships—making good ones possible.

When You Get Married, Everything Changes

Written to the love-confused Corinthians, 1 Corinthians 7 is Paul's summary on the topic of marriage. For the Christian, the primary problem with marriage is not finances, communication, or what to do about children. The problem with marriage is that you're *married*. Once you are, you're going to act like it, work like it, and think like it. Worse, you're going to be concerned about it and really devoted to it, and that's no good because you're about to be divided. That's a killer—don't let it happen.

Because time was short for the Corinthians (and is for all of us), Paul continues in verse 30 by writing that as for "those who mourn, [they should live] as if they did not; those who are happy, as if they were not; those who buy something, as if it were not theirs to keep; those who use the things of the world, as if not engrossed in them. *For this world in its present form is passing away*" (1 Corinthians 7:30-31).

The world we live in is transitory. It's terminal, but we're not. We're not of this world, and we don't live for it—we live for something else, and that's what's threatened.

Paul continues his train of thought in verse 32:

I would like you to be free from concern. An unmarried man is concerned about the Lord's affairs—how he can please the Lord. But a married man is concerned about the affairs of this world—how he can please his wife—*and his interests are divided.* An unmarried woman or virgin is concerned about the Lord's affairs: Her aim is to be devoted to the Lord in both body and spirit. But a married woman is concerned about the affairs of this world—how she can please her husband (1 Corinthians 7:32-34).

What's the problem? Marriage and our concern for it! Paul doesn't want that for us because it draws us too deeply into the affairs and distractions of this world, dividing us between the world we're from and the world we're in. That's a terrible way to live! He writes, "*I am saying this for your own good,* not to restrict you, but that you may live in a right way *in undivided devotion to the Lord*" (1 Corinthians 7:35).

Marriage (and all relationships, for that matter) may easily become the thief of singular devotion to Jesus. That's Paul's startling point. The conclusion he gives to the Corinthians is that the right way to live—the Christian way—is in *undivided devotion to Jesus.* That's how you and I live and find true life. It's the new normal! If you and I do not live that way when we're with our spouses, let alone with everyone else, we're restricted, bound-up, robbed of Christ's ability within us, and left to something else—a performance.

Here is a question to consider: Would you rather have Jesus' love for your spouse and for the people around you or your own? Would you prefer yours or your tagalong's?

Living in undivided devotion to Jesus ensures that they get His love—and that you do too.

God Is Love

You and I know that God is love (1 John 4:8,16). He doesn't just have love. He doesn't feel more loving one day and less the next. He doesn't offer love to those He finds particularly loveable. He *is* love. Malcolm Smith writes that God is the source of love:

I may tell you that I have a glass of water or a reservoir of water, but it is an entirely different category to say that I am water! To have water means that my possession of it is subject to change whether by increase or decrease, but to be water means I am never subject to change because it is what I am! He is the definition of love; love is the way He is.*

Genuine love comes from God. When you were brought into a favorable relationship with Him, you immediately began to know and discover real love. Relationship with God is the only relationship that can produce authentic love. That's why we become so devoted to Him—we do it for love! And it's a high compliment when we do.

No matter how good every other relationship is, it cannot produce love—it can only stimulate love. A weekend at a cabin by the lake with your wife elicits love and rekindles it, but it cannot *produce* love. Perhaps you've noticed that the longer you go without truly knowing God's love for you, the more dried up your love is for others. Given enough time without it, you resort to dredging up some memory of love in order to act out what was once living within. But you know love is missing. Even though you are devoted to those around you, you're approaching empty, and only a return to God for who and what He is—love—will bring about the power of true love.

The wonder of that love is that it always extends to those around you, near and far. The longer you've been a Christian, even with all your ups and downs, the more you've found within yourself a resilient desire to know Him, the One who is and produces love. That's not a selfish desire! Indulge it! God put it there because that's the normal way to live, and it's best for every relationship you've got.

What Happens If You Don't?

Yet if you don't live for love—for God and who and what He is

---

* Malcom Smith, *The Lost Secret of the New Covenant* (Tulsa, OK: Harrison House, 2002), 58.

by sowing to the Spirit and indulging your deepest desire—you still have to be with people, and you still have to behave. Without His love alive in you, your little inner well of life will begin to grow toxic, and so will your relationships.

Here's an example of what might happen. We get with someone—our spouse or a roomful of people—and we begin to think of all kinds of questions: What would be the right thing for right now? What should happen here? How do I want to be perceived? What does she think of me? How should I approach them? What should be on my face? What about my body language? What should I say? As she looks at me, or as those in the room notice me, what do their faces say about me, and what should I do about it?

Our perceiver-expresser fills up with thoughts and feelings and a multitude of questions about what's needed or what to do. So instead of being aware of Jesus and instead of sowing to the Spirit right then, our awareness of everyone else gets bigger, and *Jesus disappears*!

We can't feel Him, we can't hear Him, and we don't know what He's thinking because we're busy feeling, hearing, and thinking for Him! Not only are our thoughts consumed by earthly things, but we've given Him nothing to do. We lose the joy of being devoted to Jesus because we're working on our devotion to others. We're more devoted to the immediate relationship—the one we can see right in front of us and how we're doing in it—than we are devoted to Jesus and how He would do in it. In our thinking, we're left all alone. That's toxic, and it's not for us.

Religion persuades us to become preoccupied with the results and benefits of knowing God but not with the reality. So we commit too soon to doing whatever we perceive would be the best thing—the thing that would get us what we want, and we miss the One who lives within. And if we don't sow to the Spirit, looking, feeling, and listening for Him, we sow to the flesh by default. You know what that means.

Satan schemes to turn us from the incredible enjoyment of the life we find in knowing and trusting Jesus to the life we believe we should have through proper employment of His principles. The life Jesus promised us is Himself, not the life of good relationships or the life of a happy home. He, who is our life, may be known and enjoyed at all times—whether happy and secure in relation to others or not, whether walking up the aisle at church or walking out the door at divorce court. Jesus is the way, the truth, and the life. He didn't say He would tell us the way to go, He didn't say He would tell us the truth, and He didn't say He would tell us about life so we could have a good one. He *is* the way! He *is* the truth! He *is* the life! (John 14:6). For Christians, true life is knowing God; everything else is a picture of life that is passing away. Speaking to the Father, Jesus said, "Now this is eternal life: that they may know you, the only true God, and Jesus Christ, whom you have sent" (John 17:3).

Christ Has What We Need

If I sow toward Him who lives in me, turning my thoughts toward Him, I'll know Him, I'll hear Him, I'll feel Him and His love, and I'll be led in some manner toward those I meet. That's life! Christ formed in me (my tagalong) treats people and behaves toward others *through me*. He knows and loves them perfectly. He is concerned for them, knows their future, and has exactly what they need. What He is and what He has is way better than what I can muster up by the flesh, and it's all available to me! And it's available to them.

Here's the terrific by-product (and perhaps the best part of it all): The burden and fear of how to say things just right, how to lead just right, and how to respond just right is lifted from me, and I'm made a free man in my immediate submission to Jesus. I've placed my confidence and hope for relationships upon Him! It's amazing how much fear vanishes from my life when my chief effort is to know Jesus moment by moment. Not only when I'm praying or reading my Bible or worshiping Him at church—but throughout the day. To me, that's worship!

Paul wrote that he wanted the Corinthians to be free from concern, particularly that which had to do with pleasing their spouses (see 1 Corinthians 7:32-34). Did that freedom from concern about how to make their wives happy mean doom and gloom for their wives? Hardly! It meant that their marriages would not reflect those of the world around them, which were tragically awful, because they would benefit from the love, care, and ability of Christ in them. He would be at work and on display, the "profound mystery" for which God designed marriage in the first place (see Ephesians 5:21-33).

To assure them that he meant the best for them and their marriages, Paul wrote, "I am saying this for your own good, not to restrict you, but that you may live in a right way in undivided devotion to the Lord" (1 Corinthians 7:35). Marriage is a devotion divider, drawing the attention and devotion of the spouse away from the Lord and the issues of heaven, giving it to the spouse and the issues of earth. If and as we are drawn away from singular devotion, the production of love suffers. What happens to our relationships when that happens? We struggle to know what to do without the One who has no such difficulties. Relational frustration and eventual exhaustion is on the horizon. Devotional division will wear you out.

You've noticed that you have only so much devotion to give. If your devotion is like a pie, you have only so much to go around. Take a wife piece here (five tips on loving your wife), a daughter piece there (five techniques to grow a happy girl), and what's happening to your pie? It's diminishing. It's divided up. Not only that, but where your devotion is given to others, expectations and demands will be placed upon it, and judgments will be made as to how effective it is. And off you'll go into the concerns and methods of this world, losing what your singular devotion to Christ had been giving you. You'll end up living again after the fashion of this world—by the flesh— and that's no way for you to live.

Singular devotion to Jesus, the life, is the way to face your day— you're going to love it. However, you probably won't master your devotion immediately after reading this chapter. You're going to fumble a bit. The next time you feel the collision of devotional possibilities around people, you may be tempted to revert to former ways of relational navigation. Getting the response you want from people by figuring out what works best will continue for some time to be a powerful motivator. But going that route means you will lose the joy of knowing Jesus, and it will cost you your freedom. You'll grow weary of the wrong way and prefer the true way. Besides, that old way of living doesn't work for you or anyone in Christ. When the divorce rate among Christians mirrors that of non-Christians, the evidence that worldly ways fail the church should be compelling.

Bill and Mary Have the Wrong Focus

It doesn't take a lot to notice how much like the world our relationships are these days. Out of understandable anxiety for the wreckage of relationships, we've been stuffing ourselves with how to be concerned for our spouses. Gleanings from well-meaning psychologists have indeed benefited many marriages, and I don't mean to suggest we shun them. However, the help received by couples is primarily at an elementary, relational level (a here's-how-to-get-along-with-each-other level) rather than a Christian one. They took Manners 101 in nursery school ("Billy, it's not nice to paint on Mary's face"), but now it's time for Manners 401. Couples don't absolutely have to have Jesus inside in order to have good relational skills, but no couple can grow in Christ without Him—and that's the goal of relationship. Employing relational skills, couples may feel better about each other and learn how to relate better (no small thing), but they don't know Jesus any better. They may be impressed with how good principles work, but they miss out on how Jesus in them actually works. It's unintentionally kept from them. What happens? Their hope remains in each other's ability to get enough tools and information in order to successfully have a relationship, as though that were the highest goal and the best place for their investment.

Let's say Bill and Mary go to a marriage enrichment seminar. They've worked long and tiring hours in order to get there, and their expectations for what they'll receive are high. In the first session, they hear lots of funny stories about couples' differences in perception, talents, gifts, desires, and hopes. There's a lot to laugh about! In session two, they're taught about their God-designed personalities, their love languages, their disappointments, and how to understand what each other means *behind* their words. It's deep. Finally, in session three, they're given the tools by which to have the caring and loving relationship they've always wanted. There might be time given to practice them and then, in the glow of vulnerability, they head home to put it all into practice. What a weekend. Only it's not long before the weekend is long gone.

In the end, Bill and Mary learned what to do out of concern for each other. Seems good, but that's exactly how the natural life of this world works—here's what you should care about, and here's what you should do. And that's exactly what Paul warns us *not* to do. Our couple has been loaded up with concern for each other and how to meet that concern with that knowledge.

It won't be long before our glowing couple will be reduced to gloom. Mary will notice that Bill has slacked off in his commitment to cherish her, and it will bother her. And, in view of his commitment failure, hers will be affected, and she'll know it. Gloom. Bill will slowly notice a withdrawn and gloomy Mary, and he will ask the obvious question: "Honey, what's wrong?"

Mary might stuff her feelings and impressions with a brilliant and convincing, "Oh, nothing." Or she might say, "I don't feel loved by you. I can't believe you've gone back so soon to the way you were before the retreat." And now, Bill joins the gloom.

It may not be precisely this way, but this is the typical scenario. Over the span of a weekend, our now gloomy couple was educated as to "how things are" and "how things work" and yet graduation resulted in a failure of love. By relying upon their educated concern for each other, love is turned aside.

And what's left are two unhappy and unwitting Pharisees who, after finding each other wanting, sleep in the same bed—near but far away. Christian growth must not become all about working smarter and better with each other. It should be about finding Christ within. Transformation must not become a self-improvement makeover. Christ does the transformation—in and out. Working as hard as they can, Bill and Mary may wind up with a form of godly relationship (they get along well enough), but they will have been robbed of the power a godly relationship provides.

Sometime in the future, one or both will probably break down and admit their inadequacy, calling on the Lord. And you know what happens then—love makes a comeback. Love from God always means love for others. What they've actually been looking for is the *result* of God's work in them. And they can have that anytime.

When Paul faced an antagonistic crowd of pagans who had never before heard the gospel, he didn't rely upon his upbringing, his training under Gamaliel, or his own savvy way of reaching some of the particularly nasty Corinthian pagans. He writes, "When I came to you, brothers, I did not come with eloquence or superior wisdom as I proclaimed to you the testimony about God. *For I resolved to know nothing while I was with you except Jesus Christ and him crucified* (1 Corinthians 2:1-2).

God's Power Triumphs Above Man's Wisdom

I don't know about you, but before I faced a dangerous crowd of unbelievers, I would be tempted to prepare a lot more than that! I'd invest in a demographic study, find out where certain parts of town were, plan to provide plenty of food and refreshments, make sure I had made my presentation tight, enlist armies of prayer warriors, and map out the quickest route out of town—just in case. But not Paul. He relied upon knowing Christ right in front of the pagan crowd, his best and highest course for action. How did his body respond, and what was the result?

> I came to you in weakness and fear, and with much trembling. My message and my preaching were not with wise

and persuasive words, but with a demonstration of the Spirit's power, *so that your faith might not rest on men's wisdom, but on God's power* (1 Corinthians 2:3-5).

Because he wasn't employing fleshly techniques but instead was relying upon the mystery of Christ in him, his body felt alarm—but look what happened! The Holy Spirit demonstrated Himself! What else was needed? Many Christians today commonly suffer from a lack of certainty that they have indeed been saved, perhaps because they were aggressively talked into it or because the appeal was so grand and perfect, but it's not likely that Paul's hearers did. *They knew* because God's power made sure they did. What a relief.

This is one of the ways by which we live "in the new way of the Spirit," and not after the manner by which those under the former covenant lived (see Romans 7:6). Unlike them, we live by faith in God's ability from within us as well as around us, and that distinction must be made so it can be lived out. We should expect Him to work within us—it's His gift and our thrill!

Since Paul expected so much from Christ within, he was able and encouraged to make himself a slave to all men. This is how and why he could (see 1 Corinthians 9:19). With God inside, what could happen to Paul outside of God's influence? And think of the daily anticipation—every encounter an adventure and each appointment a wonder! What will God do next? The will and purposes of God will be known by you because He will be at work within. And that's the Christian life.

Listening to the Holy Spirit

A couple of years ago, I was speaking to a group of wonderful Christian punker types. Perhaps you've seen some: bodies pierced, hair done up in outrageous angles and colors, and a mishmash of clothing borrowed from circus performers. They tell me that most people avoid them, which is pretty much what they want.

By no plan of our own, we hit it off. Think of it: my hair, clothing, look, and manner are conservative in every way, the exact opposite of what they would normally accept, and they are the same for me. Yet we love! Why? Christ is in us.

At the end of one night's seminar, a young woman asked if I might like to have a cigarette with her—a way to invite me to talk. As we sat down, I thought, *Holy Spirit, I am glad You're in me, ready to do so much. I love You and offer myself to You for whatever You would like.* As she talked about fairly light things, I listened with one ear and gave the other to the Spirit. A few minutes passed when I heard Him say, "Ask her how long she has been a cutter." Now, because that's a very difficult thing to approach, I again offered myself to Him and heard the same thing. My fleshly mind put up a bit of a struggle on the surface of my awareness, but I was still enjoying a deeper contentment in Him, so I asked the question. I didn't dress it up with, "Thus saith the Lord," nor did I try to make it more palatable with, "I sort of feel maybe like God wants to tell you He loves you." Instead, I calmly asked what I knew to ask.

You know what happened? Her mouth agape, she first peeled back one pant leg, then the other, and then moved to her sleeves, all the while wondering how I could know such a dark and secretive thing, especially without even a hint of condemnation or shame toward her. Scores of uniformly neat razor scars were laid bare. She had little to hide before Mr. Conservative. As her face grew flush and her cheeks wet with tears, she poured out her many tormenting fears, as well as the misshapen remains of genuine hope and love for God. Think how gloomy Little Miss Punker had been. She wanted God more than anything, but she didn't think the desire was mutual. Think what it must have felt like to find out *it was.*

She was rescued through me that night, and her faith rested with Him and not with me. But I got the thrill of the thing. Look for Him, devote yourself to finding and feeling Him, and experience the delight of His presence right in front of others. You'll be free from the tyranny of the urgent because you'll know the grace of the One who is in no hurry.

Questions for Discussion

1. According to Paul, is it a good idea to be deeply concerned about pleasing your spouse? Why or why not?

2. If knowing God were your highest goal, what would people around you say and see about you?

3. What happens when you become more aware of people around you than of Jesus? Why?

4. When Paul faced "crazy" people, what did he do? What were the results?

Chapter Ten

Friendship with Our Friend

*Does God Bother with You Because
He's Bothered or Because He Likes You?*

A man of many companions may come to ruin, but
there is a friend who sticks closer than a brother.

PROVERBS 18:24

That's what real love amounts to—letting a person be what he
really is. Most people love you for who you pretend to be. To
keep their love, you keep pretending—performing. You get to
love your pretense. It's true, we're locked in an image—an act.

JIM MORRISON

Doug is his name.

There are at least 132 people who believe they are best friends with Doug. By now, there are more. Doug is not only genuine, fun, unassuming, brilliant, and sincere, he is there *for me* in a way that sometimes makes me uncomfortable. I might be struggling to keep myself together during some trying day or circumstance, and Doug will just happen to call. Hearing the stress in my voice after I've told him how bad I've got it, he'll ask, "So how are you?" Now what I really want is sympathy. "Man! I can't believe what's going on around you!" Or I could use a collaborative offer. "I'm comin' over there, and we'll take care of this together!" If he would just run over and give me a pep talk along with an Adrenalin injection, that would be just perfect. What a friend—my personal coach and pusher.

But no. Not Doug.

He'll ask, "Ralph, what are you feeling? Why does this bother you? What do you think God is doing right now?" Isn't that awful? Who has time for that? What I want is renewed strength and clarity so I can get the job done, not an uncomfortable probe!

I might respond, "Look! I'm feeling just a little mad because things are in chaos, and God is not budging! It's as if He's just happily seated on His throne, ignoring me! I'm trying to serve Him, and He's not helping."

And Doug might say, "Yeah. I can sure understand that. It must feel exactly like that. But what are you trying to do that He won't?"

And there it is. A harpoon where I needed it—right to my flesh.

I'm suddenly aware that I've been chasing a goal like Ahab chased Moby Dick. After slaving away and pushing the crew of my own *Pequod* in order to get close enough to plunge the harpoon directly into the side of my project and thereby conquer it, I've become entangled by my efforts to slay the beast. Moby Dick has me, and, gasping for air, I've been taking an awful dunking ever since.

My friend cut me loose. I had been working way too hard at something God was not doing, but I couldn't let go of it. Whenever that happens, the real Ralph disappears in favor of an actor who can get the job done—Ralph for Ahab. His crew may fear him, but the ship does move. Whatever it takes, get the job done, right? Only I'm lost in the process. Even if everyone is serving the agreed upon purpose (to get Moby), God has little to do with it—everyone's lost.

It's right then I need a friend. Doug likes me and likes to be with me, but he insists upon authenticity when we're together. If he thinks Ralph has become a flesh bag, he is alarmed enough to help me. That way, we can get the most out of our friendship. Even though it sometimes feels like he is against me, he is all about saving me all the time, and I love him for it. His harpoons are directed at my flesh because he knows and loves my heart.

My friend is a lot like Jesus.

We're God's Friends

In our day, it's common to speak of believers as warriors, servants, and disciples. In its place, that's well and good. *We are*. Many a believer has been rightly motivated to action by such scriptural references.

However, consider that (in our desire to inspire) we may have overemphasized our warrior and servant status while neglecting our desirability as *friends of God*.

How often do we think God is seeking after us to give us much more than our orders for the front lines? Perhaps a semi-stern talking to? A calling on the carpet? A little finger-wagging in the face? Or perhaps for an opportunity for us to fess up and repent?

The Holy Spirit wrote a letter through Paul that speaks of an outlandish—even eccentric—love and grace "lavished upon us" already (see Ephesians 1:4-8), but many of us feel as though our love-crazed Groom is now hesitant concerning our impending nuptials. Like He doesn't have that look in His eye He once did when gazing upon us. It's not so, but it may be what we think.

What if God likes to be around you because He believes you're His friend? Is it possible that even though we make a big deal of being servants of the King, the Emperor Himself has something additional in view? "I no longer call you servants, because a servant does not know his master's business. Instead, I have called you *friends*, for everything that I learned from my Father I have made known to you" (John 15:15).

In this chapter, I simply mean to remind you of His opinion of you and maybe stretch your understanding a bit. Approaching Him upon the basis of what He has already made of you, drawing near to Him, speaking to Him, or listening to Him in faith about what He thinks of you is the way to invigorated life and awe. It is also the way to recognize just how much He seeks you out…to spend a few moments, to share a secret, to drive out a fear, to remove an anxiety by telling you the truth, to provide joy, love, and peace. He's really good at being your friend because He has actually made you His friend.

Friends like each other. Friends share secrets. Friends laugh together. Friends make plans together. Friends rely upon each other through thick and thin, and they are intimately involved in each other's lives. They are *for* each other.

Could you accept that God might approach you today simply because He likes you? Or because the way you encourage and make people laugh makes Him happy? Or because you notice people and go out of your way to sincerely compliment them, and that pleases Him? He likes watching you! Or maybe your style of clothing, hair length, color, or even the way you zip around the corners in your car brings a smile to His face. Could He have made you so well and so right that He likes to be with you in a way that is obvious and delightful?

Singer Wayne Watson has it right. Take a look at the lyrics to his song "Wouldn't That Be Something":

> I had this dream and You were in it,
> There was this party and You were there.
> Simple evening with just a few close friends,
> People were pressing for Your attention.
> You were patient, everybody could see,
> But all the time You were lookin' round the room for me.
> But hey, after all, it's my dream.
>
> I wanna be the kind of friend that Jesus would call,
> You know if He had a telephone.
> At the end of the day;
> Just to talk about nothin', nothin'.
> Yeah, I wanna be the kind of friend He'd wanna be around.
> You know, without a word, without a sound.
> Wouldn't that be somethin', somethin', yeah.
>
> Is that so hard to imagine,
> The Lord Jesus as a friend like that?
> Spending time in the pleasure of your company,
> True companion like no other.
> Oh, you never had a friend like this.
> If you're havin' a little trouble believing,

Come on, put yourself in my dream.
Wouldn't that be somethin', somethin', yeah.*

Friendship with God Enriches Our Service to God

God is the best at everything He does. He is loving— more so than anyone else. He is merciful—His compassionate feelings run deepest, and His helpfulness is unrelenting. He is understanding— you can never baffle or frustrate Him. He is faithful—without flaw! He is your friend—is there a better one? Nope.

In all our attempts at service and discipleship, the best ingredient is friendship with our Friend. Without it, service and discipleship become qualities necessary for employment with God, dry and measurable, always under scrutiny by the Big Boss. Did you punch your time card today? Were you on time? Did you have a pleasing attitude? Did you whistle while you worked?

Have you ever gotten tired of serving, serving, serving? What ended your fatigue? Wasn't it when you stopped and got off the job? Doesn't that tell you that something is missing in your service? There is! It's friendship with God. Ultimately, He *is* the Big Boss in the Big Office, but He doesn't confine Himself to *proper relationships* commensurate to His status, shunning interaction with the lower subjects of His corporation. He's with you! Right there on the job, sharing in your labor, delighting in your style, making much of Himself by pointing at you in front of the angels. He enjoys you!

I don't mean to demean service to God—it's just that many of us have been kept from the delight and honor of it because we're so concerned with how we're doing it and that we have to. Nowadays we commonly measure ourselves by the amount and quality of our service but rarely by the enjoyment of our friendship with our Friend.

One of the most startling things I tell people in leadership roles in ministries—with children, youth, music, women, or whatever—is

---

* Words and music by Wayne Watson from the album *The Way Home.*

that they don't have to do it. "God won't be collecting your time card at the end of this week, you know," I tell them. If service to God has become a grinding drudgery, the antidote is not more service or less—it's a renewal of friendship with God. Discovering that we can enjoy His friendship *on the job* is what keeps us well *in the job*. When serving becomes more important than friendship with Him, the life and value go out of it, and you probably know what a power outage that is.

Serving God is a high calling, and friendship with God is not the cost but the fuel. Yet if we can be sold on the idea that service is the highest compliment to God and not love reciprocated and friendship enjoyed, then Satan can soon make us weary and prevent us from discovering the full stature of our identity. Something of the glory of God gets hidden.

But what if we give ourselves to enjoying God and His friendship with us? Will we get much out of it? Will we still serve Him? Will it help us on the job and make a car payment? Yes, sort of. Friends love each other, and love works. More specifically, love invigorates and *compels* us (see 2 Corinthians 5:14). It motivates us and carries us into the day in order to see where it might rush out. It's relatively effortless, like a perfect stream moving through you. And couldn't you use a little bit of that on the job? How about around home? Or in your relationships?

Let me ask you this: If you spent a day dwelling upon and enjoying the love God has for you, would you expect to receive an infusion of power, some real "oomph" for your day? Would you expect to be supplied, pushed, and driven by it, knowing that it would be the *best thing* for your day?

We *Always* Need the Love of God

Many of us treat the love of God as though it were a rarely needed winter coat. "Sure glad I've got that jacket in the closet. I know it's there for when I *really* need it." We're even working hard *not* to need it, cramming ourselves with "how to love" sermons and books and filling ourselves nearly to death with seminars on ways to act and approach people as though love were truly compelling us. Since the Holy Spirit never condemns one of His own, I don't mean to either. Yet isn't it strange we go on our way, day after day, missing love and calling it *normal?* No wonder the practicality of learning and speaking the love language of those around you is so appealing—we have a vacuum to fill.

And you're no dummy. You're not avoiding God's love in a masochistic attempt to avoid deep satisfaction. Nope. This whole thing has been and continues to be the effort of the enemy.

I believe that we've been lured away from love and friendship with God because we've become dependent upon finding *another kind* of compelling, one which seems promising and possible for our day. We make or buy beverages to get us going (hooray for Starbucks with an extra shot!), we go to seminars to get us going, we read books and go to church to get us going, and we go to school and marry spouses to get us going. We even take vacations to get us going. Nothing is wrong with these things (except maybe a little addiction to caffeine) unless they keep us from discovering the power we get from God. And frequently they do. It's rare that we grasp how the terrific yet simple ingredients of love and friendship with God provide genuine get-up-and-go for our everyday lives. If we did, we would make knowing His love the indispensable priority it ought to be.

God doesn't *have* love. God's love doesn't ebb and flow or rise and fall, motivated by the subject. God *is* love (see 1 John 4:7-12). He looks always to satisfy His love in those who receive it. And when you and I know it, believe it, and are convinced by it, His love comes together in us and compels us to share it. That's why He invites us so much to love. I think it is His highest priority for you and me.

When we fail and break down, it's not a failure of service or of proper discipleship. It's a failure of love. And God's love is at all times lavished upon us because of His grace to us in Christ. You can know what He thinks of you and why He approaches you in the manner

He does (as a friend) because of His grace! Approaching Him as a friend will affect your life. In love, you'll look and act like a servant and disciple of Christ. With appreciated grace in evidence, you'll look great.

Augustine wrote, "If you but love God you may do as you incline." He was serious! A person in love with God will be inclined to do whatever pleases Him. That's what love does to us. And that's why Jesus summed up the law with two commands: to love God and to love your neighbor. Paul also wrote that loving one's neighbor fulfills the whole law (Romans 13:8-13; Galatians 5:14).

Here's what I suggest: Lay aside your worker-bee identity, your servant-oriented, warrior-in-the-kingdom distinctiveness, and be willing to accept a real friendship with God. Ask Him about it! You won't lose anything worth keeping, and you'll get God in a particularly satisfying way. You'll love it, and He will too.

Questions for Discussion

1. If Jesus called you on the phone, why might He do it, and what might He want to talk about?

2. Is it difficult to accept that God likes you? Why or why not?

3. Have you ever experienced burnout in your Christian life? How did God refresh and revive you again?

4. How easy is it to admit when we're not knowing or trusting in God's love? Why?

Chapter Eleven

The Eyes Have It

If You Don't Like What You See,
You're Missing Something Terrific!

So from now on we regard no one from a worldly point of view.
Though we once regarded Christ in this way, we do so no longer.

2 CORINTHIANS 5:16

Our thoughts are unseen hands shaping the
people we meet. Whatever we truly think them
to be, that's what they'll become for us.

RICHARD COWPER

O ver the last couple of years, my maturing eyesight has caused
my Bible to creep farther and farther from my face, making
reading it a wrestling match for focus. I've been feeling like a zoom
lens on a camera, searching for the optimal range as my hands hold
my reading near, then farther away, still farther away, only to exceed
the perfect distance, requiring a reversal of the whole process. Until
now, I've never had any problems with my eyesight, so I was very frustrated, and I remember thinking, *What's the deal? Why is it so difficult
to focus? Is something wrong with my eyes? I've got to be able to focus!*

Where hanging reading glasses on my face solved *that* focus problem, it brought to light a more serious issue of focus in my life: My
eyes don't tell me the truth.

Refocusing Our Eyes

Sometimes I'm confident I would have sided with the ten
Hebrews sent on reconnaissance into the land of promise, loudly

arguing with those two imbeciles in denial, Joshua and Caleb. "Did you happen to *look around*, Joshua? Did you happen to notice everyone in Goshen is a big brother to Shaquille O'Neal? I'd rather get into the ring with one of those WWF monsters than wander into *their* territory! Think of our families! Think of our future! Do you suppose this to be a wise move? You may be a big man on campus around here, Caleb, but over there, you're Mini-Me!"

Only two out of twelve had it right, but those two weren't seeing what the other ten were seeing. They surely noticed the men looked like gigantic Dennis Rodmans, but Joshua and Caleb were kept sane by the truth when confronted with what they saw. The truth was the greater influence. "Be strong and courageous, because you will lead these people to inherit the land I swore to their forefathers to give them" (Joshua 1:6). The ten who reported and wanted to live according to what they saw went temporarily insane, forgetting who they were and who was with them. Sometimes I'm among their number.

God had long promised a land loaded with good stuff for His people, and *that* they could understand, *that* they could imagine. No doubt they expected easy livin' at Resort du Promised Land.

There was just one problem they didn't expect—the neighbors.

Nobody on the block was about to respect who the Israelites were—not the Canaanites, Hittites, Amorites, Perizzites, Hivites, or Jebusites. They were wicked people, rivaling any of today's worst. If the children of God were to live next door to Ozzy Ozbourne and company, one of two things would happen: They would cling fiercely to the truth in the middle of severe opposition to it ("Do not turn from it to the right or to the left, that you may be successful wherever you go"—see Joshua 1:7), or they would let their eyes do the talking, conforming their lives to what they reported.

Well, you know how it went—*the eyes had 'em.* For much of the time, they lived *out of focus*, and I'm concerned we do too. What happened to our ancestors happens to us—we forget who we are (and who other people are) when our consistent gaze leaves the truth, and we drift toward the appeal of outward appearances, the temporal facades of the world around us. After all, that show is always on. So our eyes fake us out. When they do, our approach to life goes with them. We can't help it.

A Church in Distress

Here's an example. Let's say you've heard some particularly distressing things about a local church you used to attend. You've been told by more than a few people that there is rampant hypocrisy amongst the members, as well as lying, cheating, smoking, doping, stealing, drinking, immoral sex, and the like. They're looking ugly. For all the wrong reasons, they've even made the newspaper. Further, no one there seems of a mind to stop what they're doing—repentance isn't on anyone's agenda.

Monday morning brings a phone call from one of that church's elders with a unique request. He wonders if you've heard what's been going on at his church, and after you tell him that you have, he gives even more grimy details. He then asks, "On behalf of the elders, I wonder if you would write a letter to our congregation addressing our situation, which I will read to the church this coming Sunday. Whatever you write, they will hear. Will you?" Feeling the weight of the moment, you nevertheless respond, "Yes, I will."

So what's going to be in your letter? What do you have to say to those awful-behaving, unrepentant, backslidden believers? You'll have their attention—what do you give them?

Essentially, that's what happened to the apostle Paul, who, by the grace of God, penned his first letter to the Christians at Corinth. Like you, he had heard all about the ugly and awful behavior of the church, and he wrote a letter for them all to hear. He knew he would have their attention—what did he write?

> Paul, called as an apostle of Jesus Christ by the will of God, and Sosthenes our brother, to the church of God which is at Corinth, to those who have been sanctified in Christ Jesus, saints by calling, with all who in every place call

upon the name of our Lord Jesus Christ, their Lord and ours: Grace to you and peace from God our Father and the Lord Jesus Christ. I thank my God always concerning you, for the grace of God which was given you in Christ Jesus, that in everything you were enriched in Him, in all speech and all knowledge, even as the testimony concerning Christ was confirmed in you, so that you are not lacking in any gift, awaiting eagerly the revelation of our Lord Jesus Christ, who will also confirm you to the end, blameless in the day of our Lord Jesus Christ. God is faithful, through whom you were called into fellowship with His Son, Jesus Christ our Lord (1 Corinthians 1:1-9 NASB).

What's wrong with Paul? "*Grace* to you and *peace* from God our Father and the Lord Jesus Christ"? Is he kidding? Why would he write a thing like that? Isn't that an awfully big assumption? They were "enriched in Him, in all speech and all knowledge," and "not lacking in any gift"? And these misbehaving believers would be kept "blameless" until the end? Paul, how can that be? Can't you see what they're doing?

The Corinthian Christians were guilty of so many things, and yet Paul addresses them like that? We're able to read ahead in Paul's letter, so we know that they were looking and acting a lot like the pagans of Corinth because Paul spent the majority of his letter correcting them. They were guilty of drunkenness (1 Corinthians 11:21), of sexual immorality and fornication (5:1), of taking each other to court and cheating (6:1-8), of divorce (7), of being a divided church (1:10), of stubbornly remaining infantile in their faith and worldly in their living (3:1-3), of arrogance (4:18), and more. Don't you think Paul should have lowered the heavenly boom on them and knocked a little sense into them? Would you in your letter? Most of us would.

The Corinthians' Identity

Why would Paul, who knew all about what they were doing, and who knew more than most anyone what an affront sin is to God, first speak to them in such a way? Why not first give them a good righteous whack across their unrepentant backsides?

Here's why. When Paul thought of the Corinthians, he thought of them as they had *become*, not as they behaved. He lived by faith, not by sight (2 Corinthians 5:7), and that framed every view for Paul.

He knew that if they were acting in ways contrary to whom they had become, it was because they had forgotten whom they had become! Paul's first duty was not to correct their behavior, as if to say, "Stop that, you cruddy Corinthians!" Instead, his task was to awaken them to their faith in the God who had made them sons and daughters!

Paul approached the Corinthians not with a behavior-curtailing whack but with an attempt to draw them back to worship. They needed revival more than they needed restraint! The Corinthian Christians looked ugly and did ugly things not because they were in fact ugly, but because they had allowed their thinking to become ugly. They had forgotten the majesty of God's mercy to them in Christ (forgiven!) and the incredible change He had made for them (new creation!), and their behavior made it obvious. When faith is dormant or sickly, who looks particularly good? What's needed is the truth that revives.

Paul does the same thing in his letter to the Romans:

> Therefore, I urge you, brothers, *in view of God's mercy*, to offer your bodies as living sacrifices, holy and pleasing to God—this is your spiritual act of worship. Do not conform any longer to the pattern of this world, *but be transformed by the renewing of your mind.* Then you will be able to test and approve what God's will is—his good, pleasing and perfect will (Romans 12:1-2).

Without the proper "view of God's mercy," no believers will rightly offer their bodies, and none have any particular reason to worship, no matter how we might scold or prod them.

The Corinthians' behavior was awful, but it had not changed whom they had become. So in faith, Paul appealed to that. Instead of first giving them restrictions, he gave them revival. Instead of conforming them to a proper look, he built them up in Christ. His purpose was far higher than behavioral correction. How is that different from what the world does? Paul believed the Corinthians had been made sons and daughters of God, so his first target was transformation through the renewal of their minds, not by the correction of their behavior.

His focus was riveted upon the unseen because that's where true life is understood, and from that focus, Paul approached whatever he encountered. Because their behavior was so awful, it was obvious to Paul that while his focus was secure, theirs wasn't! So he directed their thoughts back to what God had done for them and what He thought of them—all in the unseen. With that in focus, with God's opinion restored in their thinking, they could begin again to live by faith! They could see what Paul could see.

See to the Heart First

I am not saying behavior is unimportant: Rather, I am saying that our *way* to behavior is vital. If, as Paul wrote to the Galatians, "it is for freedom that Christ has set us free" (Galatians 5:1), then perhaps the worst thing we can do for behaviorally ugly Christians is to curtail their freedom by introducing restrictions *before* reintroducing them to awe-inspired worship and renewed faith. See to the heart first.

That has been my approach to believers for more than 20 years now. Whether speaking at a church, to a small group, or with one person in a café, I assume Christians are in a nearly constant, invisible war for what defines life. The devil and his demons strategize that believers should identify themselves and others according to what they see and nothing more, but God and the angels work for them to believe they and others are what God says they are—and nothing less. The battle for the Christian is over whether life is defined by what they see or what they know. Battle lines drawn and faith hanging in the balance, are people defined by how they look, behave, and perform, or are people what God says they are—even if we can't see their true identity outwardly? How we approach them will reveal what we believe, and it will determine our success.

I like to be around well-behaved people, but my goal is not to work in such a way that they become what I like. If I teach the church I pastor or the group to which I'm speaking or the person at the café how to look good and behave well, I might be successful, but so what? That counts for next to nothing! What matters is a new creation (Galatians 6:15) and how Christ is being formed in us (Galatians 4:19).

You could be a Mormon, a Scientologist, a Buddhist, a Jehovah's Witness, a Christian Scientist, or a Pantheist and concern yourself with manners and good behavior, but what would it matter? Not a thing. The measure of a Christian is not first how he behaves, but who is taking form in him! That might make for some sloppy behavior while he learns to sow to the Spirit and allow Him to produce life, rather than to live after the old way of the written code. But it's the way to live!

The Prodigal Son

And that's God's approach. When the formerly lunatic, prodigal son returned repentant to his father, Daddy didn't say, "Well, before I welcome you back, do you promise to behave? To get along with your brother? To treat your mother and me with respect, like the Bible says?" He did not. To Dad, his boy was an honored son when he left with all the loot, and he was the same when he returned looted. Who had the right focus? Daddy's eyes saw his boy, a filthy, smelly mess by his own doing, returning from "a long way off." But did his eyes capture and direct him? No! The truth controlled Dad ("my *son!*"). And Dad, overwhelmed with compassion, ran to his boy—"Let's get that pig stuff off you!'"—and embraced him with unbridled affection.

Dad was not focused on what his son must have been involved in, given his appearance, but on the deeper truth—his birth. In the terrible confusion of strong messages to the contrary, being controlled and directed by the truth will keep you focused and walking in faith. *Control* is a strong word, but sometimes our eyes and flesh might lead us to a fleshly response: "Idiot! You spent all my money, pig boy!" It's then that we want to be managed and influenced by the truth, remaining in its control and living by faith, not by sight.

Before the son could make any commitment to a change in behavior, his father restored him to the security of who he was in the family all along—perfect royalty! And the son found himself by looking into the eyes of his father, who saw the truth.

> But the father said to his servants, "Quick! Bring the best robe and put it on him. Put a ring on his finger and sandals on his feet. Bring the fattened calf and kill it. Let's have a feast and celebrate. For this son of mine was dead and is alive again; he was lost and is found." So they began to celebrate (Luke 15:22-24).

We live in a time when thousands of prodigals (some secretive and some in the open) live terrible lives all around us. How many Christians do you know who have run off with their inheritance from Dad and embraced a lifestyle far below what is in keeping with who they are? When you see them, what do your eyes tell you? Usually it's something like, "They shouldn't be doing that. They shouldn't be living like that. They should be going to church. They should be glorifying God. What's wrong with them anyway?" I will tell you: They've lost their minds, they've lost their senses, and they're acting like it.

When you close your eyes and think of who they actually are, you're beginning to focus. Then, by approaching them from there, you can help the temporarily insane. You don't have to tell them it's against God's will to feed and lie with pigs. *Revive them!* Help them come to their senses! Like the prodigal and like the Corinthians

(2 Corinthians 7:8-16), they'll awaken from their demonic stupor, throw off the sin which so easily entangles them, and glorify God by worshiping Him anew. "Oh, Father! I am what you say I am—perfect royalty—not what my eyes tell me I am! What do I want with the stuff of this world?"

Seeing People for Who They Are

This is why we set our hearts and minds on things above, not on earthly things (Colossians 3:1-3). We don't focus upon the unseen so we'll feel better and have a happy day; we do it because that's where we find ourselves in relation to God and to each other—*really well off!* From that focus, our lying eyes cannot lead us astray and foul our approach to life.

When we see people, particularly Christians, we'll see them for who they truly are, and our relationship with them will be profoundly affected. For, like us, they've been crucified with Christ and have been raised with Him, righteous and noble sons and daughters of God, no longer of this world and no longer accurately regarded by its point of view—*particularly by other Christians.* Besides, it's much more fun! Would you rather be the behavior monitor of the world (regularly disappointed) or the purveyor of revival (frequently in awe of God and His children)?

If you accept only what your eyes tell you, particularly about people, you'll soon wonder why the thrill of being a son or daughter of God has leaked from your heart. In my years of pastoring, that is one of the top reasons wonderful, holy, perfect sons and daughters begin to falter and lose vigor—they believe what their eyes say about the neighbors. When they do, they cannot approach them in faith, so their Christianity becomes relatively impractical and paralyzed. They're drying out because they're out of focus.

Keeping the Focus Accurate

My digital camera takes great pictures, capturing glee on the faces of my daughters, reproducing the smile I love so much on Sarah, and revealing beautiful, intimate details of Colorado wildflowers. However, the camera has no close-up focus of its own. In order to get an accurate close-up, I have to move my entire body nearer to or farther away from the object or person in order to get in the right position for the best view and picture. More than once, I have returned from a mountain trip and hooked up the camera to our television for the family to enjoy the pictures I've taken, only to groan to discover that a stunning wildflower was blurred by improper focus. It ruins everything—there is no joy, and there is no way to rectify it. Before long, the memory of that flower in all its splendor has faded, soon to be forgotten.

I think that happens to us when somewhere along the line, for some reason, we stop adjusting our lives in an effort to get the most accurate and revealing focus. Oh, we may continue to act well, to ask for God's blessings, and to do pretty good things, but *who we are* loses its power because we can't see anymore. But we must.

Think of the apostle Paul, who, having discovered whom he had become in Christ, spent years among the unloved, unlovely believers of his day, convincing them they had been made *far better* through Christ (see Colossians 1:28-29). What a struggle that must have been! Those chosen of God, bought and remade by Him, no doubt wrestled with the ever-offered lie that they were still the ungainly misfits of that day. They might as well fit in as best they could. Paul knew better and worked to see they did too.

> Once you were alienated from God and were enemies in your minds because of your evil behavior. But now he has reconciled you by Christ's physical body through death to present you holy in his sight, without blemish *and free from accusation—if you continue in your faith*, established and firm, *not moved* from the hope held out in the gospel. This is the gospel that you heard and that has been proclaimed to every creature under heaven, and of which I, Paul, have become a servant (Colossians 1:21-23).

What a great truth to tell the Colossians. But maybe you know how it goes when, like them, you lose focus and forget God's opinion of you and of others, seeing only what your eyes tell you. Your faith fails, and you are no longer "free from accusation." When you see a believer (or yourself) do something or behave in a way contrary to who they (or you) are in Christ, you may forget who they (or you) are in Christ—and move away from the gospel, no longer continuing in your faith. Every little hurtful or evil thought about you ("I'm terrible!") and about others ("They're terrible!") will grab and hold your attention, drawing you away from the eternal truth of who people are in Christ. And your efforts with people will follow along with those accusations because you will have been moved from the gospel.

A Helpful Reminder

But you don't have to move. Try this: The next time you see a Christian, look beyond what you can see. Look to what God says is true of him (since He made it happen!) and tell him about it right then and there. "Hello, my friend. Isn't it amazing that as you stand there, you are a holy son or daughter of God, a blameless, radiant, and righteous friend of His? While you're stuck in the chaos and turmoil of this world, you are not at all *of* it, and it is not worthy of you. I know who you are, and I'm thrilled with God because of you."

Watch his face—his faith and focus will be revealed as you accurately describe him. Two things will likely happen: Either he will smile and happily embrace what you've shared ("Oh, thank you for reminding me!"), or he will frown and disagree ("Well, I'm not so sure about *that*"). Either way, you're turning his thoughts to what God thinks of him, and that's worth a little fuss. If your Christian friend has been in anything like the same fight for faith you've been in, you may safely assume your approach to him is rescuing him. He really does not fit with the ten spies whose eyes alone had them, but with Joshua and Caleb, who were focused by faith. So gently press on because you know that for everyone, the gospel "is the power of God"

(Romans 1:16). What God thinks of us has power when we believe it; we will feel it, and our renewed focus will give us a revival.

And do you wonder about spiritual warfare? This is its true launching point. Think of the harm you've done to the devil and his plans. You haven't simply given a bewildered believer a weapon or two (something to *claim* and something to *proclaim*) and told him how to use them. No, you've awakened him to who is with him and who he is—what a triumph that is! He doesn't just know how to work a weapon and swing a sword. He knows his perfect fit with God—what can prevail against him? Nothing!

I imagine Joshua and Caleb could have outfitted the deluded ten with as many weapons as they wanted, and they still would have refused to enter God's promise. What they saw had flooded out what they at one time knew—God was with them, and they were His chosen. But they were deluded about the land of promise because their eyes had them. But not yours.

Reforming Our Habits

We don't commonly think about life according to the invisible realm, so I want to make some suggestions. For the most part, we've become accustomed to a pattern of living that seems to work and "get us by" in our relationships with people. In other words, our eyes control us—we see something and act in keeping with what we see. It's a habit. If you're going to break out of the pattern and approach people as they truly are, you'll need to intentionally do something to see through the facade that confronts you and to prefer what's invisible—that's what you're all about.

Consider turning away from watching TV every night, which inoculates us against the invisible by giving us a big dose of the visible. Read the New Testament instead because it draws us into the real world, which really is for us. Resist the urge to act according to what seems normal or usual in common situations by pausing and sowing to the Spirit. Living by faith in God's opinion is an exhilarating exercise you can do all day long.

You may want to think of some situations in which you can prefer the invisible by rejecting the visible. Perhaps you've treated someone in a way that seems right and gets the job done but that now seems anything but sufficient. How might it be different? How might you approach those you know are Christians but whom you've never thought of as holy, blameless, and righteous sons and daughters of God? There they are—right in front of you. What might be different the next time?

Grow accustomed to relying upon the unseen when you're with people. They probably won't see what you do, but they can—they need to. You might even pray as Elijah prayed for his unseeing servant so long ago:

> "Oh, my lord, what shall we do?" the servant asked.
>
> "Don't be afraid," the prophet answered. "Those who are with us are more than those who are with them."
>
> And Elisha prayed, "O LORD, open his eyes so he may see." Then the LORD opened the servant's eyes, and he looked and saw the hills full of horses and chariots of fire all around Elisha (2 Kings 6:15-17).

Questions for Discussion

1. Have you ever scolded yourself because of your own bad behavior? What was the short-term result? How about the long-term result?

2. How useful might it be to think of people as they have become in Christ, rather than how they behave?

3. Why do we set our hearts and minds on things invisible and heavenly rather than on things visible and earthly?

4. What are some changes you might make in order to see past the facade of the visible, the thing that blinds us to the reality of the invisible?

Chapter Twelve

Aliens Have Landed

*The Proper Care and Feeding of the
Everyday Foreigners in Your Family*

Dear friends, I urge you, as aliens and strangers in the world,
to abstain from sinful desires, which war against your soul.

I PETER 2:11

It is the unseen and the spiritual in people that
determines the outward and the actual.

OSWALD CHAMBERS

O h, I hate school! Why do I have to go, Daddy?" Having recently
returned from an idyllic family time in Jackson Hole, Wyoming, Ellen was venting her frustration about starting the school
year.

Emma, ever the opportunist, offered her own timely impression
of a cyclone. "Yeah! I hate school too! It stinks! And I didn't get the
teacher I wanted either. I don't want to go!"

The two storms merged into a gale-force hurricane: "*Waaaaah!*"

It was category 5 in my house. In the face of ferocious complaining, I considered fleeing to higher ground—every man for himself.
Or maybe I should just raise my voice, show 'em what a *real* hurricane is like, and shut down their miserable whining—snuff out the
storm and restore order to my home. Yeah, that's it…that'll work.

But it misses what's really going on. God was at work in my
daughters, and I was a tad slow in recognizing it.

Each day that Ellen and Emma navigate the masses of moms and dads shepherding their little ones to their classrooms, they enter a realm that not only fails to recognize them but that instead assaults them. No matter how student-friendly the classroom, no matter the good rules given for respectful relationships, no matter the kindness of the smiling teachers, my daughters spend five days a week as aliens in a foreign world. How torturous! How frustrating!

Having been born from above, Ellen and Emma are as alien to this world as Jesus was (John 17:16), and it shouldn't surprise me when they feel it. *They must!* And they do—thank God. What if they didn't?

What God Thinks of His Children

Much has been written about how to foster and secure the good behavior of our children as well as how to educate them so they will be successful in life. Today there are countless volumes of material aimed at educating parents about the requirements and costs of properly raising their children. It will take devotion, time, commitment, vigilance, fortitude, and a clear plan to raise obedient children.

But is that really the goal? And what if I occasionally get lazy? What if I blow up or break down now and then? Or what if my kids don't respond properly to my maxims—just how far do I go toward insisting they acquiesce? There may be times I can't tell the difference between them being rebellious and them having warranted frustration with me. Is there ever a time I let up on them and allow them to do what they want—would that be so bad? And if I have toe-the-line kids, whose behavior is beyond reproach from school to market to church, but I have no true heartfelt intimacy and fellowship with them, that's not really success. What will I have raised— well-behaved women who know how to behave and live with a Pharisee? My girls could grow up to be women who relate to God on a similar basis.

Here's my confession: I regularly fail to do everything right with my kids. I don't mean to make light of failure, but fortunately, doing everything right is not my goal. I want them to know God—that's my goal. More than to do well and be successful, more than to fit in and be liked and well behaved, I want them to know God—where He is, what He thinks, how He feels, and what He is doing. I want that. And since my children have been made into His daughters, I must agree and begin with what He thinks of them and approach them from there. *God tells me who my children are.* I believe Him and move from that point. Anything else gets in the way.

The primary struggle my children have is the same as mine—to believe what God thinks about them and to live from it.

The biggest difference is one of experience. I have years of navigating this world's identity offerings (sports star, genius, Don Juan, pastor extraordinaire…) and found that each of those identities required too much and returned too little. Even after the shocking joy of discovering who I am in Christ, still the lure to morph into something more valued in the eyes of this world proved at times irresistible. My glance down the memory lane of 50 years reminds me of how thrilled I was at the intersection of God's revelation, but that hasn't meant a straight road following. I've looked all over the place for an identity I liked and could work best to my advantage. The identity supermarket of this world has filled up my cart, and it takes serious effort to throw out the false selves collected there. They're not me! But they're so convenient…they've come in handy before.

Our Kids Need to Know Who They Are

My daughters aren't so loaded up, though. Ellen and Emma will have to walk the same worldly aisles as Sarah and I do, where all the desirable identities available to everyone are screaming, "Choose me!" from the shelves. If they don't have as their foundation who they already are, the odds are great they'll begin filling their carts. I did.

This is not to say that all we want to give them is a healthy self-esteem. Often the response of the church to the perceived fragileness of its children is to strongly advocate that we do our best to make our kids feel accepted, loved, and properly led at home so they'll do well when they leave it. We've majored on boundaries, discipline, quality time, follow-through, and the united front presented by Mom and Dad. None of these things are wrong, but all these things together fall way short. They are prescriptions for life without answering the question: Who am I in this life?

In my formative years, I failed to ask that question because I didn't need to know.

All I was concerned about was getting what I wanted and avoiding what I didn't want, and I could do that by putting together the proper list of methods and techniques sure to get me there. I was entranced! And who wouldn't be? I was of this world, and I was intent on playing its game. I didn't approach life as though I already *was* someone, but as though I was on the way to *become* someone.

The world seemed to say to me, "If you follow these steps, you'll become the 'you' you want to be," which meant, in essence, I could do well and be worshiped. What a trick! Be a sports star, and everyone will rank you at the top. Be a genius, and everybody will marvel at your intellect. Become a Don Juan and everyone will know you're "it." Be a pastor extraordinaire, and the gathering crowd will knowingly nod as you pass by. You got it. You made it. Only what you've *got* covered over who you *are,* and your arrival obscured your beginning.

If learning how to live and applying yourself to that is ranked ahead of *who you are* in this life already (whether you're eight or eighty), your days will be spent loading your cart at the identity market. You'll labor to construct a "you" which will work in any scenario, a facade that you can slip on as the need arises. What will haunt you is that your persona—your "you"—will fail and be found out. With worldly success and admiration your goal, fear will become your silent motivator.

This early pattern for life is what usually brings confused and frustrated Christians to the later goal of weaning themselves off this world. By then, it takes Herculean effort. Season after season, year after year, we've given ourselves to what makes life work best, and when God works to mature us in keeping with what He knows is true, we feel as if He is against us. *Why isn't my life working?* comes the question. We've been sold a way of life without the definition of life.

Christian Kids Are Aliens, Just Like Us

Our Christian children are aliens. If they don't know it, or if we only teach them techniques to be successful in this life (as though that were Christian), we've set them up for frustration. When I see a trained monkey wearing children's clothing and playing with children's toys, I think it's cute, but I'm not confused. It's not natural. I don't leap and exclaim, "Wow! The monkey has become a kid! What shall we name him?" In the same way, as I train my children to function in this world, the fact that they are not of this world must always remain clear—to them and to me. They're from another. If they don't know it, their deluded attempt to fit with this world will make monkeys out of them.

Our Christian children are lights in this world, holy and blameless sons and daughters of God in whom lives the Holy Spirit Himself. They're not on a long and winding path to their destination—they've *arrived already.*

Do you see them? Not if you're looking at them only with the eyes in your head and not the eyes in your heart.

> I keep asking that the God of our Lord Jesus Christ, the glorious Father, may give you the Spirit of wisdom and revelation, so that you may know him better. I pray also that the eyes of your heart may be enlightened in order that you may know the hope to which he has called you, the riches of his glorious inheritance in the saints, and his incomparably great power for us who believe (Ephesians 1:17-19).

The "glorious inheritance" in our children right now is more fantastic than anything else in this world. Just because it isn't easy to see is no reason to turn away and quit looking! The need for revelation is another of God's invitations to know and be satisfied by Him, to be transformed into His likeness. When the Spirit reveals to me what He thinks about Ellen and Emma, I believe Him and approach them from there. In other words, I look and feel a whole lot like Jesus because I'm living by faith! And any opportunity to do that is wonderfully satisfying—it fits who I am.

If we don't know what He has in mind when we look at our children, we'll invent something instead, and it will never match up. We "live by faith and not by sight" not only in God's promises but also in what God says He has already done for people and made them to be. We see all of life according to His opinion.

Who my daughters have become is fantastic, but if they don't know it, the odds are great that they'll get lost in this world, believing they are merely humans who are favored by God. I cannot tell you how many times I have heard Christians say, "Well, I'm only human" as an excuse for some failure or frustration. Having been thoroughly educated in this world's pattern, they think of themselves as human first—*merely man*—and sons and daughters of God second. Flesh rather than spirit. However acceptable this thinking has become, it is not accurate, and it should be corrected.

Since there was "jealousy and strife" among the Corinthian believers, Paul, knowing exactly who they were in Christ, rebuked them for behaving so "fleshly," and for "walking like mere men." (See 1 Corinthians 3:1-3 NASB.) We might say today, "Hey! You're not like that. You're not just human anymore, so knock that stuff off. You've been changed into something far greater."

Violators of the Satanic Worldly Order

Every believer, regardless of age, is as foreign to this world as was Jesus. Christians don't even have to open their mouths, and they're targeted for spiritual terrorism—they're marked in Christ (Ephesians 1:13) and have become violators of the satanic worldly order. Surely that explains much of the conflict we have in it; we are being identified as permanent strangers to the system (see John 15:19). The extent of our attempts to conform ourselves to it will be the extent of the contortion of our true God-birthed image and identity—twisted, we will not work well! Neither will our chosen, changed, and believing children.

Jesus prayed for those whom the Father had given to Him:

> I have given them your word and the world has hated them, for they are not of the world any more than I am of the world. My prayer is not that you take them out of the world but that you protect them from the evil one. They are not of the world, even as I am not of it. Sanctify them by the truth; your word is truth. As you sent me into the world, I have sent them into the world (John 17:14-18).

Wow. My Ellen. My Emma. In this world, it gets no better than them! But there isn't much support of God's opinion of them to be found in our world.

Our public school system is not set up to accurately equip our children to know who they are. I don't mean to lay blame, but I do mean to illuminate. Public schools lump saved and unsaved children together and identify them all as mere humans in need of skills for the life they can have. *Here's what you'll need. We'll identify it for you.*

Obviously, they aren't going to tell our Christian kids who they are in Christ.

There's So Much More Than the Three Rs!

I want my children to learn the three Rs and to have a healthy immersion in music, history, philosophy, and so forth, but I don't want them to believe that's all there is. "Now fit in and find your lifelong career path! You can really be somebody if you'll go this way in the big picture we've set before you." That's the wrong-headed pursuit of trivial nobility, and it will lead them down a path of frustration. It doesn't fit with who they are.

So Sarah and I are ramping up our discussions about the unseen nature of the frustrations they encounter. It keeps us believing what God thinks of our daughters (we see them!), and it's illuminating and practical for them. How we see them and what speaks most to us about them will determine how we treat them. It must.

I have spoken with hundreds of parents who would tell you that they made the biggest impact in their relationship with their children by seeing them as God sees them. Prior to that, when asked to describe their kids, they would go on about what their children liked and disliked, how they behaved and didn't, and what some of their hopes and fears were. None of them said, "Well, Ashley is a female human who has B positive blood running through her veins, DNA that has produced brown hair and green eyes, a slight excess of teeth and a strong jaw, and a lineage that will probably cause her to excel in mathematics and have poor people skills. We believe she'll be quite happy working in a laboratory. Yep, that's our Ashley." No one ever described to me each physical component of the child they were feeding and raising at home.

However, no parents have ever told me who their children were from God's perspective either. "Well, Ashley is quite a lot like her Father. She's a righteous girl, full of the Spirit, and perfectly designed for His glory. We know that Ashley is of God, and we're delighted to be her parents." *His opinion* had not become *their opinion*. They were focused upon the Ashley they could see instead of the Ashley who lived within.

As long as parents see their children as people to raise and train who require shifting measures of love, compassion, sternness, strength, direction, and discipline, they don't actually see their kids. Instead, they see *trainees* who require from them the just-right combination of leadership so they can grow up and be successful, happy, faithful, and good. Therefore, the faith of Ashley's parents is wrapped up in how they are doing with their trainee: Ashley, God's little ball of clay left to their charge.

If Ashley takes cookies without asking, you had better correct her quickly so she'll know not to do that as an adult. Who knows? At 17, she might be stealing Cadillacs if you don't. If she thanks Mom for dinner and asks to be excused from the table, affirm her and praise her so she'll do that when dining at someone else's home. If you don't, she might think you don't care and become a habitual dinnertime offender. If Ashley gets a little (or a lot) snippy with you, correct her on the spot so she'll know to respect adults. If you don't, Ashley might become a snippy snob for the rest of her life, and she'll have you to blame for it. Horrors!

Absolute vigilance is what's required, and perfect parental skills are the tool. Come to this class, read these books, go to that seminar, and you'll have what? *Good kids.* Which will mean what? *Good adults.* So what? That's not what they are, and that's not nearly what they will become!

What Does God Want for Them?

God's purpose for them is far greater than whether they get along in class, do well in school, find good jobs, or become upstanding citizens in a world in need of role models. Because His purpose and plan is much higher than those things, He has already changed them. They won't "get there" sometime after middle school, high school, or college—*they've already arrived!* And they're in a nasty, very confusing storm. By His grace and through the truth, our girls will know the nature of the storm in which they live. Your children should too.

Our kids are aliens. That is an incredible fact, *and it's going to hurt,* which is why they have a built-in need for us. Intimacy with my daughters does not come from the daily Bible-teaching I'm supposed to do with them, and it does not come out of any moral instruction I may have for them either. I achieve intimacy with them by sharing in their uncomfortable and impossible fit in this world. I know the terrible struggle, I know the tempting lure, and now they do too.

It hurts. But the pain keeps us from depending on the false

comforts and techniques of this world that would cover up and diminish our "alienness." Knowing why our fit in this world hurts makes the pain understandable and perhaps tolerable. The pain Sarah and I have is the very same pain Ellen and Emma have, and it's there for a reason. When I forget who I am, that pain eventually gets my attention so that I repent and go back for a reminder.

I can't simply *treat* my kids as God would. I must *think* of my kids as God does. When I see what He sees, I fit with Him and feel it! When I do not, I give Him some work to do—on me. Our Christian children are aliens, and we live together in a land that's not our own. If we can get that, our approach to them will be vastly different and uniquely invigorating, and it will keep us living on the edge of the visible and invisible. And for us, that's pretty normal.

The devil wants our "alienness" to seem impractical. If we fall for that, we will remain undetected to ourselves, deceived from knowing how incredible and valuable we are. That's the scheme against us and our children. As soon as we're born again, our new identity marks us for the grace of God, but it also marks us as targets for the enemy—and he is merciless. The best strategy of the devil is the one least noticeable, the one which slowly ensnares its victim. It's even better if the victim likes the fit.

Raising Children in the Knowledge of God

While the Holy Spirit, Sarah, and I work to raise our girls in the knowledge of God so they can really live, there is a carnival of activity vying for their attention and allegiance. The big attractions are which television shows to watch, which fashions to wear, which recreational activities to choose, which video games to play, which foods to eat, and which boys to like. That's because visible life all around them demands their attention.

The more opinionated my girls become about visible life, the less opinionated they become about invisible life. The more Ellen and Emma grow passionate about how to clothe themselves, the less they care about the clothing they have already in Christ (see Galatians

3:26-29). The more engrossed they become in what makes up the right boy, the right food, and the right game to play, the more deeply they dive into the pursuit of trivial nobility. That's the snare. If the visible world becomes my girls' dominant passion-lighter of life, they will exchange true life for a fake. And the cover-up will be complete. Getting them to make the proper exchange later can prove terribly difficult because their expectations will have been lowered. They will try to appease their appetite for the bread of life by stuffing themselves with bread that does not satisfy.

We won't win by dressing them in frumpy duds, forbidding them to like boys, or throwing the television into the trash. We believe we are working in concert with the Spirit when we are building them up in Christ by reminding them who they are and pointing out what friction with this world really means: They are incredible aliens! We don't want that covered up. They're not *only human*—they're *alien*. It takes discipline to remember their "alienness" because the devil daily lies to them about their identity.

If we're not careful to live by faith, we might begin to sow to the flesh of our kids. One day Emma said, "Daddy, I'm a worrywart."

And here's what I thought: *You know, she is. She's always got something negative to be concerned about, and there's always some wrong or some bad that gets her attention. What a worrywart. I should tell her to trust God.* Before giving my verbal agreement along with a healthy prescription for the problem, I nevertheless paused, hesitating ever so slightly to see if the Spirit might interject something. Lo and behold, He did.

She's no worrywart. She's often plagued by it, but it's not her. It's something against her.

Shocked into the reality I cannot see, I said, "Emma, my girl, do you think that worry comes *from* you, or does it come *at* you?" Because I wanted her to think (and sow to the Spirit by doing so), I said no more.

She answered, "It comes from the monster. It comes from my flesh. Then why do I worry so much, Daddy?"

"Well," I replied, "it isn't your fault. Our monsters are really monstrous, aren't they? Everybody's is. But you and I get to see God in us, smacking the monster for us. Remember how to think or talk toward Him when you feel all that fight going on inside? It's fun to find Him in there, isn't it?" Pulling her onto my lap, I said, "Come on. Let's find Him inside together." She wiggled her little body into a comfortable spot, and I prayed, "Jesus, Emma and I believe You're in us right now. We feel the fight You're having with the monster. Would You put it in its place, and would You do what You love to do in us and make peace, trust, and love more obvious than worry? Emma and I don't like the battle inside, but we know what to do about it. Thanks for living in us."

And Emma said softly, "Amen." What a moment that was.

Clearing Up the Confusion

I don't want Emma to get overwhelmed by confusing her flesh with herself, which means I have to make that distinction too. That confusion is so destructive. The effects stretch out like roots to touch everything they can. Not only might she come to believe *she is* what God believes *she is not*, but she might come to act upon it and live out her days trying either to conquer herself or give in and give up. And that can stretch through families and friends—even to generations.

So here's what we do:

First, Sarah and I believe that Ellen and Emma were chosen by God, and that makes all the difference. We work with the Spirit to maintain not only the belief that *they* were chosen by God but also that *we* were chosen by God as well. In our conversations and in prayer (together and apart), we regularly bring up the fact of our security because God chose us before He made anything or set any of it in motion (see Ephesians 1). We were His idea, and we frequently return to awe, thankfulness, and rest because of that. It sets us right.

Everybody in our house has been made holy and blameless and

has been set up for "the praise of his glorious grace" (Ephesians 1:6). We work to make certain that we remain impressed with God's grace to us in Christ. It flavors much of what we talk about, and believing it influences and gives power to all of our subsequent choices. We live by faith in Him, and knowing that He chose us for Himself keeps us invigorated.

In my view, the church has been overemphasizing our need to choose God (and keep choosing Him) in all we do: "Kids! Do the right thing! Make good choices—*God is watching!*" Many Christians often make behavioral appeals—if kids think God is in the room, they'll be good. We have been working so hard to get our children to make good choices that I don't think we're much impressed by God's choice of them. *So we don't marvel.* We don't wonder at our kids because we're not convinced that He is convinced they're so wonderful. We need to be.

Christian Kids Are Not What They Do

Second, surface activity gets our attention, but it doesn't always reveal what's below. In 1980, I was visiting a number of churches, not knowing what I was looking for because I was a neophyte Christian. Sampling on Sundays gave me an important opportunity to see the incredible diversity among churches—their themes, theology, styles, and services were dramatically different, and I didn't know what was right or what I wanted.

Sampling one Sunday, the pastor held up one of those plastic lemon-looking containers of lemon juice and said, "Christians are containers. If you squeeze them hard enough, what's inside will come out." The remainder of his sermon was all about making certain our behavior glorified God, no matter the squeeze life put upon us. Obviously, I've not forgotten his object lesson, but my opinion of it has changed.

I want to remember and to help my daughters know *it's not true.* Likening ourselves to plastic lemon juice containers or tubes of toothpaste assumes that for any given container, there is only one item inside. Once you squeeze it, *whatever* comes out reveals the reality within.

Following that logic, if Ellen says something critical about Emma, then that must mean Ellen is a critical person. And in the critical moment, I might say, "You're such a critic, Ellen!" If Emma throws a tantrum because she's not getting her way, that must mean, "Emma, you're such a tantrum-throwing person!" Maybe I should follow it up with a nice, "Quit that and glorify God!" On the other hand, if one of them does a good deed, that must make her a good-deed doer. "Oh, Ellen, my little good-deed doer. Here's my approval, and while I'm at it, here's God's too." And all the time I would wonder just who my kids are because I would be looking only at their surface.

Do you see what happens? It's not long before life in the Harris home is all about behavior! I set myself up as Pharisee of the house, as the ever-watchful-and-critical judge of behavior and referee of results. And since I'm doing so much, God has little to do. What a happy family *that* makes.

Our Christian children are not how they behave, and they're not what they say—they're who God says they are. Without excusing poor, fleshly behavior, we must not allow it to sell the lie that our kids are how they look. When the surface looks particularly stormy, we must know that under the waves, something is amiss, and we need to go there. If our children's flesh is on display in all of its ugly glory, we must rescue them! Revive them! Build them up in Christ, remind them of how Christ has made them, and make sure they know He is in them. If their behavior is stinky, it's usually because their thinking is too. You can help them and interrupt the game against them.

This is liable to seem so impractical and impossible—so pie-in-the-sky—but *only because we've never done it.* We're so immature here that we think it's impossible. And if we feel that it's impossible, then the scheme of the devil remains effective. But you can do it—you can interrupt the enemy's game plan.

As I've said before, sometimes you simply have to stop fleshly behavior immediately: "Jeremy! Stop this instant! You may *not* put that knife in your brother!" And you may not always stop the behavior *just right* either. That's another story. But after you've got the knife away from him, take a moment to address the heart. You may assume it is being held captive as the flesh does its thing.

Our Kids Are in Christ, and Christ Is in Them

Third, Sarah and I work to believe Ellen and Emma are in Christ regardless of their behavior...no matter what happens. *That keeps us sane!* When the storm blows in our family (from without or within), the flesh often wars against the Spirit. Sometimes, instead of sowing to the Spirit, I go out and control the storm. In other words, "Do something" replaces "Know Someone," and off I go. I'm not always quick to return either.

Have you noticed that by seeing too quickly to the storm, you lose any knowledge of Christ in you—of who He is and what He has to offer? The threat of the storm and the fear it brings out of your flesh become more captivating: "Oh, no! Do something!" I'm reminded of the furious storm that blew up around that godly bunch gathered together in the boat on the lake (see Mark 4:37-41). Ever find it strange that Jesus rebuked them for waking Him up because of their fear of the storm? The disciples had first given themselves to the storm instead of to the Lord. Terrified, they had become engrossed in it. Who wouldn't? They hadn't forgotten that He was in the boat. They had simply become more involved with the threat of the storm. The disciples' approach to Him was late and out of sequence. As usual, Jesus did something about it (hooray!), but they needlessly became subject to what they saw rather than who they knew.

Through every difficulty, failure, or triumph Ellen and Emma experience (or cause us to experience), they are still at all times in Christ and have everything because of it. Jesus is their strength and righteousness. Sarah and I work to keep that foremost in our thinking and approach. We work to keep that secure foundation in our girls' thinking as well. And we're careful not to send them any confusing, false message that tells them they don't already have everything in Christ—they do! We want to be so positive about God's grace to us that earning God's favor and blessing remains something Jesus already did for them—and not something they have to do for themselves.

We know some people will say we're giving them a license to abuse the grace of God. We believe we're holding them *to* His grace and keeping them in awe because of it. We'll take the risk.

Consider Paul's thoughts on this subject:

> For *the grace of God* that brings salvation has appeared to all men. *It teaches us* to say "No" to ungodliness and worldly passions, and to live self-controlled, upright and godly lives in this present age, while we wait for the blessed hope—the glorious appearing of our great God and Savior, Jesus Christ, who gave himself for us to redeem us from all wickedness and to purify for himself a people that are his very own, eager to do what is good (Titus 2:11-14).

What is it that teaches our girls best? *The grace of God.* God's grace is not only the *condition* in which we stand with Him but also the *power* by which He works in us. Knowing God and how well-off they are with Him through Christ *works* and *teaches* our girls to say no far better than any list we could come up with and drill into them.

Talking to God About Our Children

Fourth, Sarah and I regularly talk with God about our girls, asking Him about His opinion of them. He shows us that Ellen and Emma are godly already—right on course and right on time. When their words or actions are not in congruence with who they are in Christ, we believe nothing has changed. You may assume correctly that we talk with Him a lot!

If we don't ask Him to show us what He sees, we may begin to think that God isn't doing anything with them and that they must be blocking Him. Someone is to blame—let's figure out who or what it is and get it fixed. We may begin to think of them as having a small inner compartment where God is hunkered down, cowering or embarrassed. Instead, we should see them at all times as daughters of God who are in Christ, chosen and happily indwelt by Him.

In truth, Ellen and Emma aren't just on their way to heaven—they're already *from* heaven (see Ephesians 2:6). God is far more active with His children than we are! Because we don't always see it, *we ask*.

Furthermore, we ask ourselves questions: Are our girls learning about Jesus from us? Or are they getting a heavy dose of the Ten Commandments because we just want them to be good? Are they getting shepherds who enjoy walking with them or Pharisees who walk with them only to keep them in line? Shepherds enjoy intimacy, while Pharisees sacrifice it for a proper performance. Are we truly enjoying our girls, and are they truly enjoying us? If we get stung by such questions, we head into some focused time with God, who has the grace and love to set us right.

But what if it doesn't work? What if our little aliens don't live by faith? What if they don't make the right choices and follow God? What then? Then we'll be living by faith in God—we have no other plan.

> All these people were still living by faith when they died. They did not receive the things promised; they only saw them and welcomed them from a distance. And they admitted that they were aliens and strangers on earth. People who say such things show that they are looking for a country of their own. If they had been thinking of the country they had left, they would have had opportunity to return. Instead, they were longing for a better country—a heavenly one. Therefore God is not ashamed to be called their God, for he has prepared a city for them (Hebrews 11:13-16).

Questions for Discussion

1. Can you see how the world has offered to you a "you" that has led you away from the real "you"? How does that affect you?

2. If you have or know some Christian children, what will it do for you to think of them as alien—just as alien as Jesus?

3. How does it make you feel to know that God chose you? How will that affect your life?

4. If Christian kids are not what they do but who God says they are, how might that affect your interaction with them?

Chapter Thirteen

The End of Pretending

Receiving Frustration's Gift to You

But we have this treasure in jars of clay to show that this
all-surpassing power is from God and not from us.

2 CORINTHIANS 4:7

No matter how discouraged we get, God has
not asked us to do the impossible.

GEORGE GRACE

There are lots of ways by which to know and feel and hear and
experience God. I've found that any way I can know Him and
find Him in me is worth it. And while I have my favorite ways and
cling to them (wading in a mountain stream at sunset while waving my fly rod would be one), there are some other ways I'd rather
avoid and just read about. These are the ones that would not be my
first choice, but they may be the most important.

A friendship I had long trusted in went steadily wrong some
time ago. No amount of phone calls, e-mails, meetings, and prayers
could clean up the mess. My one-time friend was determined to cast
me as his enemy. Not even my silence put out the fires of accusation,
and the ugly smears went on without me. Even though it boggled
my mind that there was nothing I could do, I brooded on it still,
turning it over and over in my thoughts, even in my sleep. I was terribly frustrated. It was the ugliest battle of my life.

God was surely doing something, but I wanted Him to do
something else. I wanted Him to make things right, to trumpet my

innocence and integrity, and to do a great work in my friend's heart. It didn't happen, and I'm not holding my breath.

This is what *did* happen: I found God in me. Finding God in me is an experience I love most, but it sometimes comes through something I love least—personal anguish. Because I had to, I turned to Him, looked for Him, listened for Him, felt for Him, depended upon Him, and knew Him in my terrible state of frustration. Months of ongoing battle went past, and I understood anew what had at times been only theory: "When I am weak, then I am strong" (2 Corinthians 12:10). I loved knowing God in that season, but I would still hesitate to sign my name when the "Who wants to be treated like Jesus?" volunteer list came around again.

My personal rallying cry has to be what Paul wrote to the Philippians in chapter 3—I cannot get enough of knowing God. I remember the joy of discovering that knowing Him was truly my biggest thrill and greatest desire. I was so happy! But I also read that my favorite mentor not only wanted to "know Christ and the power of his resurrection," but also this little phrase: "and the fellowship of sharing in his sufferings" (Philippians 3:10). While my early days of delighting in Jesus went on and on, that little tidbit still occasionally haunted me. *Jesus suffered a lot,* I thought, *and it was sometimes horrible; it was always unjust, and it was often alone.* My inner coward worked out an alternate route. "Maybe if I have great integrity and solid character, work hard, and am really nice, fun, and good to have around, I'll escape that suffering part."

Riiiiiiiiiiiiight.

I don't like suffering. I have worked long hours at building a doctrine against it. Am I not supposed to prosper in everything, be in good health, and have a fair portion of those "cattle on a thousand hills"? Isn't that the deal? Isn't that what I got when I signed up?

Working the Spiritual System

When I first became a Christian, the majority of the teaching I got was about how to work the spiritual system. If you do it right, you get good things; if you do it wrong, you get the opposite. Whatever happened that was good and that made me prosperous and happy was from God (proving you were doing something right), and whatever happened that was bad or ugly or frustrating was from the devil (proving you were doing something wrong).

Simple. Work the system.

Because I wanted good, I worked hard to do the right things and began urging others to do the same. "God wants you to live well so it will go well with you, and here's how." Work the system. Simple.

The only difficulty I was having was that I read my Bible. And when you've got neat and tidy, user-friendly doctrine like I did, you're going to be troubled by the Bible, especially when you hang out with Paul. "For it has been granted to you on behalf of Christ not only to believe on him, but also to suffer for him, since you are going through the same struggle you saw I had, and now hear that I still have" (Philippians 1:29-30).

Really, Paul, what a bother you are. If I had to listen to you, I wouldn't fall asleep and fall out a window like brother Eutychus (see Acts 20:9-12)—I'd *jump*.

Come on—*work the system*. Simple.

Unfortunately (or fortunately, depending upon how you look at it), I continued to read my Bible, and one day I stumbled across a passage that the Holy Spirit would use to forever upset my smug assessment of life.

Paul's Thorn in the Flesh

In his second letter to the Corinthians, Paul wrote of an incredible time with God that essentially equipped him to be something of a know-it-all. Now knowing a lot isn't a bad thing, especially if one were to have the assignment of preacher to the Gentiles. Yet, after reporting an amazing (and no doubt satisfying) time with God (2 Corinthians 12:1-6), Paul writes, "To keep me from becoming conceited because of these surpassingly great revelations, there was given me a thorn in my flesh, a messenger of Satan, to torment me" (verse 7).

What? I thought. *Where's the sense in that?*

After a moment, the following question popped into my mind: *Who would want to keep Paul from becoming conceited?*

Answering the sudden pop quiz, I thought, *Well, not the devil—he'd* want *Paul to become conceited. It must have been...oh, no! God gave Paul the thorn? God intentionally weakened Paul by giving him something demonic? Does that mean God was against Paul? It can't!* As my tight theology began to unravel, I read on:

> Three times I pleaded with the Lord to take it away from me. [*Only three? What if Paul had asked a fourth time? Would that have worked?*] But he said to me, "My grace is sufficient for you, for my power is made perfect in weakness." Therefore I will boast all the more gladly about my weaknesses, so that Christ's power may rest on me. [*God wanted Paul weak, so does this mean He wants me weak as well? And He works in my life so that happens?*] That is why, for Christ's sake, I delight in weaknesses, in insults, in hardships, in persecutions, in difficulties. *For when I am weak, then I am strong"* (2 Corinthians 12:8-10).

Oh, no. This changes everything, I thought. And I was right.

That day I backed up and read the entire book of 2 Corinthians in one sitting. I vividly remember feeling painfully refreshed, as though my brain had just been slapped with aftershave. *Thanks. I* needed *that.* After my Corinthian glut, I wrote the following in the empty margin of the last chapter: "God will not rest until you do. He will burn you out."

Sooner or later, you're going to come up against a terrible weakness you cannot avoid—the lure of alcohol, pornography, cheating, gorging, or coveting—and it will be too strong to resist. It will be a frustrating inability you're unable to conquer, an unjust accusation that won't go away, a public insult that marks you and wounds deeply, or an impossible hardship or a difficulty you cannot weather. So you'll cry out to God to rescue you, but He won't. You'll still have the weakness, you'll still stumble, your situation won't change, you won't receive an apology, and things will remain unbearably difficult. And you'll be right on time.

God Uses Suffering

In virtually any kind of suffering, God works in us to bring out what He put in—the very life of Christ. God lives in us, and even though it's a pleasure to find Him there in safety and prosperity, it is at least as important to find Him there in calamity and poverty. It's terrific to have God at a party where everyone is celebrating, but how much better to have Him at a disaster where pain and chaos reign? Think how He would stand out.

And that's what He likes.

I want to live by faith in what Jesus said is true about situations and people—good and bad, those who are His and those who are not yet His. Living by faith means that I believe His Word and choose to carry out the kind of actions in keeping with it, including trusting Him and treating others in a manner that glorifies God. The energy necessary for the acts is the beginning point of finding Christ in us.

We're prone to pretending, you and I, acting as though we're capable. But in truth, we're not. God has not invested Himself in our capability, but in His own. And He wants you and me to have that. God is not willing that we should be kept from the authentic life and grace of Christ in us, so He allows and sometimes even causes awful frustration to visit with us.

This isn't about learning and growing either. Once you've found Christ's power at work within you through frustration, it doesn't mean you've passed the class and that there will be no more tests. What a crazy thought that is! We expect that as we grow in Christ, life gets better with time, we pass one class and grade after another, and one day we'll graduate. That's not what this is. This is where belief and experience meet, where life is less and less about pretending and posturing and more and more about the reality of Christ in us. Paul's life experiences didn't get better and nicer or become mellow with age. He didn't proclaim that he wanted to be done with this life and get on to the next because he was bored—it was because he ached. (See 2 Corinthians 5:2.)

Prolonged frustration and bother don't happen simply to goad us into good behavior or to teach us a lesson—they keep us from pretending we can do anything apart from Christ. And such things happen so we'll find Him. The inability to keep yourself together or to keep producing the look of love for someone for whom you feel none is not a sign that you need to recommit and do the right thing. It's meant to show you that you cannot (and are not supposed to) do anything apart from Jesus. Frustration is the beginning of the end of pretending.

Remain in Christ

Too often we fail to think of ourselves as *in Christ*, living in Him at every moment. Instead we think of ourselves as *outside of Christ* with a whole lot to do for Him. We may think of quiet times and moments of solitude with Jesus as charging up our depleted batteries. "Better not let yours run down too far, or your whole system will crash," we say. "Plug in, charge up, and off you go. Hope you're charged up enough to face the unknown of the day. And when it appears you're not, keep smiling, hold it together, and pretend anyway. Wouldn't Jesus want it that way?"

No, He wouldn't. Instead, in light of your inability, He would beckon you to live by faith that He is within and that He is capable. That's why frustration is so important! It keeps us bothered with this world and the stuff we go through every day so we'll not live by it or for it. When you've grown discontented with the world, a look within will save you from a needless burnout.

Here's how Jesus put it:

> Remain in me, and I will remain in you. No branch can
> bear fruit by itself; it must remain in the vine. Neither can

you bear fruit unless you remain in me. I am the vine; you
are the branches. If a man remains in me and I in him, he
will bear much fruit; apart from me you can do nothing.
If anyone does not remain in me, he is like a branch that
is thrown away and withers; such branches are picked up,
thrown into the fire and burned. If you remain in me and
my words remain in you, ask whatever you wish, and it
will be given you. This is to my Father's glory, that you
bear much fruit, showing yourselves to be my disciples
(John 15:4-8).

When we try to do much apart from Him, we become "like a
branch" that is good only for the fireplace. We're just heat that passes
away.

How many times have you witnessed people doing a lot for the
Lord, people really "on fire," only to watch them burn out? Usually
the fire doesn't die out in a moment—it tends to happen over a season of time. Flare-ups happen here and there, but they happen less
and less often until finally the fire is out. No matter how the hearth
is poked and prodded by the pastor or by friends, the heat is gone.
These people are like dry branches.

That's when one of two things happens: Some people, having
grown cold, will settle and grow accustomed to their state, saying,
"Well, the honeymoon had to end sometime, didn't it?" Sometimes
they continue to regularly fill their seat on Sunday, smiling and responding appropriately, departing with a look of satisfaction. They've
learned to get by and to deal with the sad lack of heat, now mostly a
haunting memory. They'd like more, but getting their hopes up will
just lead to disappointment, so they don't muster the strength they
think is required. They're present, but there isn't much heat.

On the other hand, many burned-out Christians evacuate the
building, limping off disappointed and disillusioned. Someone failed
them, but they don't know whom to blame, so they slink off, never
to be heard from again. Why should they be subjected to one more

"Here's what you've gotta do for God," when it doesn't work, or they just don't do it? Having heard their share of sermons as to how to act busy (as if they had fire and heat when, in fact, they don't), they weary of pretending. If you ask them why they left the church, they tell you, "All the people there were a bunch of actors, and I can't do that anymore." To them, going to church is like joining the Screen Actors Guild, in which some who have joined can act, but others (like themselves) can't and refuse the stage, wandering off dejected. That's what these do. In either case, it's cold because the fire's out.

God, Our True Fuel

Burnout is all around us. When I speak of burnout, I don't mean to say, "The limited amount of fuel in the fireplace of our heart has been consumed! So let's replace it and get that fire burning again, wiser and smarter, with more potential for a long burn." What I mean is that one kind of fuel has finally been exhausted—burned out—and it's time for a *new kind of fuel* altogether. God Himself is the fuel for our lives.

Today the media is crammed full of information about alternative fuels. From uniting gasoline with big batteries in our hybrid cars to finding new ways to energize our lives, fuel for energy is everything. "Can't stay awake at work? Nodding off too soon? Drink this potion, pop this pill, eat this energy bar, do this workout, and voilà! Strength!" But that kind of strength can become a stand-in for true strength from God, and it won't work—even if we think it will.

God knows who we have become, so He works to exhaust our singular reliance upon false or insufficient resources (charisma, style, eloquence, talent, strength…) so He can be found and formed in us, becoming visible through us. What's more exciting than that? And He does it whether we recognize His effort or not—with or without our permission. *And* He will use just about anything in our lives to bring it to pass, including pressure, conflict, and disappointment—not only on the job, but also at church or with a spouse. He may use physical frustrations, heavy burdens, relational craziness, and even a messenger of Satan. Out of gas? Feeling exhausted? That's *good*. It's time for a new fuel source. God is that faithful, and we desperately need Him to be.

Just when you would think God would pave the way and make things easy for Paul, the opposite occurs. Out preaching the gospel, Paul writes, "We do not want you to be uninformed, brothers, about the hardships we suffered in the province of Asia. We were under great pressure, far beyond our ability to endure, so that we despaired even of life. Indeed, in our hearts we felt the sentence of death. *But this happened that we might not rely on ourselves but on God*, who raises the dead" (2 Corinthians 1:8-9).

Paul, do you mean it happened on purpose? Yes. Did God have something to do with it? Yes. God will so orchestrate things in our lives so that we cannot cope, notwithstanding the energy drinks, alcohol, pornography, drugs, recreation, and therapies that we use to medicate ourselves. He is *not* punishing us! Nor has the devil broken through God's protective boundary unauthorized, now to ravage our lives and plans. This is not a call to "suck it up" and muster the proper strength so God can do something, but an invitation to proper weakness so that Christ's power may rest on you as it did on Paul (2 Corinthians 12:9). Only then is God's grace discovered to be entirely sufficient. God had set Paul up to find Christ within, and He was working with Paul so he would. That usually takes some doing.

My Christian history shows that I don't quickly embrace weakness in order to find God. Suppose the Spirit sent me an early morning e-mail about my day that read, "Good news, Ralph! Today will be a terrific day of weakness—you'll have opportunities galore!" I think I would suddenly come down with the flu and jump back in bed! I would rely upon fleshly resources, and looking out at my day, I would fail to look within. And that day Christ would not be found in me because I would have found an alternate way to live and cope—staying home.

Have you ever done something like that? Have you ever been

faced with an upcoming meeting you knew would be difficult, and instead of looking and listening for God in you, you gave everything you had to be properly prepared? Did you dress and psyche yourself up, put your name on the prayer chain, plan out several options, and cross your fingers so you could handle anything and everything? How did you feel afterward? Exhausted? You burned the wrong fuel.

God thinks He lives in you and that you would love to find Him there. He wants to reduce your stress by relegating you to more of a spectator than an initiator. God is carrying on the process that will get you off the demanding stage of life, taking away all the pressure you feel to come up with today's best act and resources to match, so that He can provide what He is like in you. In essence, He is working for intimacy with you and intimacy with the world through you! Everybody gets Him.

Finding Christ in Weakness

This is how God treats us—not as sons and daughters only, but as vessels for Himself, holy containers for His show. God didn't make me and choose me so I will do well—I was chosen so He will do well, and He made me and chose me so that it would be *obvious*. That's the part that makes me feel like it's not always a good idea to cuddle up with God. My flesh, recoiling with horror, makes itself felt. "Quick! Do something! Say something! Don't be a coward and do nothing—move!" But more and more, I'm learning to prefer what God thinks. That may seem foolish and weak in the opinion of this world, but I'm no longer of this world, and I know better.

Besides, God has been choosing the foolish and the weak for a long, long time. He didn't stop before He picked us either, so you know what that means—count us in the crowd. Why would He do that? Well, where would God be most visible and obvious? Wouldn't it be where things are tough? Wouldn't it be in situations and circumstances where, in contrast with how things appear, He would stand out?

Think about what Paul told the Corinthians:

> For God, who said, "Let light shine out of darkness," made
> his light shine in our hearts to give us the light of the knowl-
> edge of the glory of God in the face of Christ. *But we have*
> *this treasure in jars of clay to show that this all-surpassing*
> *power is from God and not from us* (2 Corinthians 4:6-7).

Just try thinking of God lurking in a planter, and you've got the
picture. Should the pot attempt to be strong and capable, summon
its mineral resources, and put on a show? No! It should take every
opportunity to fall over! It doesn't have a mouth, so it can't invite
anyone to take a peek inside. It doesn't have talent, so it can't dazzle
anyone enough to prove what's there, and it certainly can't defend
itself against a hammer: "Boy! We've given you a dozen whacks, and
you haven't cracked. God must live in there!" It's not that we actually
are jars of clay, but figuratively speaking, we each have one within us.
Now that God lives there, every knock and smack on us is an invitation—not to parade the pot, but to crack or tip over, letting out
the treasure! The whack on the pot will happen again and again (like
it or not) because God loves to work through you and me. We get
delight (*God is in me!*), and others get the life of God.

> We are hard pressed on every side, but not crushed; per-
> plexed, but not in despair; persecuted, but not abandoned;
> struck down, but not destroyed. We always carry around
> in our body the death of Jesus, so that the life of Jesus
> may also be revealed in our body. For we who are alive
> are *always* being given over to death for Jesus' sake, *so that*
> *his life may be revealed in our mortal body.* So then, death
> is at work in us, but life is at work in you (2 Corinthians
> 4:8-12).

Doesn't this shed light on why things happen the way they do?
God is moving us from one resource to another. As He exhausts
our natural resources so we can live by faith (call it *brokenness* if you

must), He is carrying on with the sanctification of His sons and daughters. God is orchestrating for your life and His life to meet! When we know what He is doing, we can look through the temporary and visible circumstances and live by faith, finding the grace and energy of Christ in us.

I think Paul majored in this. Do you want to serve Jesus? Consider Paul. His life of serving the Lord included being whipped with 39 lashes on five different occasions, bobbing around in the ocean for a day and a half, being beaten with rods three different times, being shipwrecked five times, being stoned by a mob, and being on the wrong side of jail bars! I tend to whine and fuss about my life not going the way I want if a publisher rejects my manuscript or if my car doesn't start immediately, but Paul saw life differently. He was better off because he did (see 2 Corinthians 11:24-29).

Do We Just Need a Good Whacking?

Some people think they are stubborn and resistant pieces of cement that God can hardly wait to break. They might imagine the Father saying this: "Jesus, do whatever it takes to break Ralph Harris—he's just so hard-hearted. I can't use him until he's broken!"

"Yes, Father, I see what you mean. I'll work up a plan and get the angels on it right away. He's a tough one, but we'll get it done."

Those who think this way often explain the circumstances of their days along these lines, as though the One who had rescued them was now the One resisting them. Rubbish. Everyone born again by the Spirit has been born of a new nature, and they have everything in keeping with the terrific new creation they have become. At the core of their being, they will never again be unyielding pavement, nor will they have a rebellious spirit, nor will they need to be broken. If believers believe that they have a rock for a heart, then they will interpret most every hardship or difficulty in their day as God working to bust them a good one, getting their attention and securing their allegiance. "Knock that off, son, or I'll *really* give it to you next time!"

Giving my dog a whack to her backside might send her a message, but *she's a dog*, and we don't speak the same language, we don't have the same nature, and I don't live in her! I may get the behavior I want (and the lowered head and tail between the legs as well), but so what? Do I get any glory for what I've done? Any worship or praise? Is she glad and thankful for the whack? No! She just wants to do whatever it takes to avoid it in the future. Is that how God treats us—like His special pack of dogs? That's a dog's life, but it's not mine, and it's not yours.

Performing the Parade

Some in the Western church think that in order to get God the notice He deserves, we ought to throw Him a parade, complete with blaring bands, cheerleaders, and oversized balloons. And as we march by, decked out and heads held high, those along the parade route (and those watching on TV) will certainly witness the glory of God in our splendor. Right? When the onlookers see how good and clean we look, how well we march, and how tightly we keep our formation, they'll want to join in too. So we've got to practice our moves and work on our routines so that when it comes time for the show, we'll be ready and hit the right notes. We'll be prepared and strong, and we'll have it all together.

But that's not how it works.

For as long as I've been involved in ministry, I have experienced the competing desires of the parade versus the power of the kingdom. I expect disagreement on this point, but the two do not get along. Almost without exception, people are best met and changed by God Himself not during the glamour and power of the parade but in the privacy of failure, in the distress of weakness, and in the torment of frustration. That's where God is, and the people who know Him best find Him there and continue to visit.

Hardship, suffering, and trials in the life of a Christian do not arrive because we're bad but because we're good (see James 1:2-4; 1 Peter 1:6-9; 4:12-19), and God is at work showing everyone just how good He has made us. God, who lives within us, loves to put Himself on display through the behavior of His vessels. Some will disagree, but I don't believe that God rebukes believers for sins they've committed by trashing their days. I think He directly speaks to them about it. If we sow to the flesh, we will reap from the flesh the junk Paul lists in Galatians 5, but we won't be reaping it from God. Naturally, if I spend my days in pajamas drinking bourbon, watching television, and cussing out the neighbors, my life will be miserable. But it won't be my Father making me miserable—it will be the flesh! As soon as I wake up from my worldly stupor and repent, God takes up the recovery of His sloppy-behaving son. He's really great with prodigals and the temporarily insane—He's amazing.

This keeps us from losing hope and letting go of faith and desire for God when the situations and circumstances of our lives are not what we would like them to be. Isn't that incredibly important? If we think we're the ones responsible for all the hardships, why bother turning to God for any insight and encouragement? What's He going to say? "Too bad about all that frustration. Better resolve yourself to unending misery, you big loser."

But that's not what's going on.

> Therefore we do not lose heart. Though outwardly we are wasting away, yet inwardly we are being renewed day by day. For our light and momentary troubles *are achieving for us* an eternal glory that far outweighs them all. So we fix our eyes not on what is seen, but on what is unseen. For what is seen is temporary, but what is unseen is eternal (2 Corinthians 4:16-18).

"Light and momentary troubles" don't arrive simply because you've failed, because God is mad at you, or because the devil is on the loose. Even if you've messed up mountainously and are reaping what you've sown to the flesh, your foolishness and weaknesses are still opportunities for the Lord Jesus. Try to eradicate them from your life, and you'll compound them! Look through them and see them for the whacks on the pot that they are. Sowing to the Spirit, you'll decline the energy you're tempted to muster for the strength and ability He has.

And you won't be pretending. You'll start appreciating your weakness because you'll find the energy and life you're meant to have—Jesus Christ in you, the hope of glory!

> Dear friends, do not be surprised at the painful trial you are suffering, as though something strange were happening to you. But rejoice that you participate in the sufferings of Christ, so that you may be overjoyed when his glory is revealed (1 Peter 4:12-13).

Questions for Discussion

1. Do you have an "inner coward"? If so, has it kept you from knowing God? How?

2. Are you prone to pretending? What good has come of it?

3. How could weakness save us from burnout?

4. Why do "light and momentary troubles" come to us? What's the point?

Chapter Fourteen

Stripping Mummies
Finding Freedom and Life Outside the Tomb

The dead man came out, his hands and feet wrapped
with strips of linen, and a cloth around his face. Jesus said
to them, "Take off the grave clothes and let him go."
JOHN 11:44

The main thing between you and God is not so
much your sins; it's your damnable good works.
JOHN GERSTNER

On a cool and damp full-moon November night many years ago, a good friend and I were strolling on the docks of an ocean harbor. Such places light me up because I have so many good and vivid memories attached. Since I was nine years old, my dad took my brothers and me on lots of fishing trips, many of which began in predawn hours at a harbor gateway. Loaded down with fishing rods and tackle boxes, the walk to the boat was an exciting sensory smorgasbord. Dim lights, salt water, drying nets, rotten fish, and the smell of diesel engines mixed together in a promise-loaded greeting that meant something great was about to happen.

It was the same on this night.

As we walked, my friend asked me about a recent event that he thought must have hurt me. He assumed the situation had left me deeply disappointed. Gathering myself, I said, "Well, yeah, a little, I guess. But I trust in God." He responded with a therapeutic "hmm" and instantly decided to join the ranks of people who bother Ralph. Most would have just left my comment alone and moved on to other matters, such as the weather, work, or the new cars I thought were cool. But he began presenting me with hypothetical situations where I, the central character, would be the target of mistreatment. After each fiction, he asked a very bothersome question: "How would that make you feel?" Each time, I took a moment to assemble my best "Christian" answer: You know, the kind that sounds *wise* and *nice*.

The final scenario he presented to me had me on an elevator along with one other guy. After the doors close, the man turns toward me and spits in my face. With no explanation offered, the man quickly exits at the next floor. "How would you feel?" my friend asked.

Summoning my Christian resources, I answered, "Well, I'd be shocked." Because that wasn't enough of an answer, I added, "I'd wonder why he did it. I'd wonder how I could minister to him, since he was obviously in turmoil. I'd wonder what his family life was like, what his relationship with his father was like. Stuff like that," I said.

Brilliant.

But not enough to placate my friend. "So you wouldn't be angry? You wouldn't be mad?" he asked.

"Well, sure. I mean, who wouldn't? But I'd be more puzzled than angry." Applying more pressure, my friend asked if I would have only a little bit of anger, just a smidge. Suddenly, I felt deep within me the smallest flame of anger—like a pilot light. Warm, but not enough to heat the house. Now I was in trouble. I was caught in the crossfire of two threatening realities: Anger is not Christian, and neither is lying. So I admitted the flame while trying to contain it. "Yes, I suppose I would be a bit upset…a little embarrassed."

"So you'd be angry then?" he asked.

And I exploded. "Yes! *Yes!* I'd want to rip his stinking head off, *okay?* How dare he do that to me! What a *jerk!*" I yelled.

Immediately heaven threw open a door for an instant. Like the shepherds terrified by the sudden presence of heralding angels centuries ago, we recoiled as everything around us lit up in brighter-than-daylight illumination. For a split second, we could see every house overlooking the harbor and every moored boat. Everything was clear to us in the cameralike flash of the moment. And two life-changing things occurred: First, God revealed His love for me. The not-so-Christian rage I felt didn't deter His thoughts and feelings for me in the least. I was freed that night from the imprisoning fear of needing to hide and pretend with God. His love for me comes without restraint, and it is not lessened by any bad thing I feel or do.

The Bible is true after all.

The second thing was that I saw something else besides the solid structures and vessels before us. I suppose it was a vision from God, a message He wanted me to have beyond any form found in this world. In the nearly blinding light, I saw a sort of chalk drawing on a dark background, an outline of an upper torso. No head, no legs. The left arm hung straight down, while the right arm was crossed at the elbow in such a way that it reached up across the chest to the left shoulder. I had no idea what it meant. But unlike Joseph, who waited many years before God revealed what the vision of stars and grains bowing down meant (see Genesis 37–50), I waited only 13 months until God staggered me with the meaning.

During an everyday, run-of-the-mill conversation about nothing in particular, God suddenly revealed that the torso was *me*. In less than a snap of my fingers, I knew about my whole life, my angled right arm showing the approach I took every day—I blocked anyone and everyone from getting to my heart. I never let anyone in, and I never came out. I was afraid of what people would find and the damage they might do if they got too close. So I became a facade, a human projection screen. I was a put-on, surviving by projecting the appearance that would get me what I wanted. I was pretty good at it too.

But God, being who He is—insert all the "omni" words such as *omniscient, omnipotent, omnipresent*, and so on—thinks He's in charge of His Spirit-birthed children. So a kind of floodlight revelation was in order. God doesn't have to be satisfied when my form of

Christianity is not to His liking, no matter how good it looks, even if I'm okay with it. *Turn on the light.*

Taking the Mask Off

As if to permanently affix the meaning in my heart and mind, the day after God explained the vision to me, I was to speak at my school's retreat on the theme "Mask Busters." It seemed to those of us on the planning committee that telling each other how to live without putting on worked-up personalities or inflated attitudes would be a valuable thing. I was well prepared with Greek and Hebrew definitions to impress my fellow students and faculty, thereby convincing them. (Do you suppose there was a mask there?) However, what they got was me blubbering about how much people scared me—and how much I needed them nevertheless. I told them my story. Some of those who heard me became far better friends because I had been genuine and confessed my fleshly penchant for a cover-up, and they assisted me toward an open and authentic life.

My desire to either impress people or avoid criticism induced me to a performance—a life on stage with an audience watching. I learned long ago that if someone asked a question in class that sounded dumb or was something everyone else already knew, that person would be ridiculed with sneers, frowns, gasps, and giggles. A blown pass, a missed basket, an embarrassing moment in front of girls, a bad grade posted in public, a job rejection—all were to be avoided or covered up. On the other hand, a witty statement, a moment of insightful commentary, a good game, and a girlfriend were the gold coins of success. People were watching. All that meant a covered-up way of life. It's how I grew up.

After I became a Christian, what it meant to God was an impaired life. I wasn't living—not as a Christian, anyway.

Fortunately, God was determined to get rid of that needless cover-up. Little did I know that He would send people to assist me toward a new kind of life, a reconciled and happily uncovered way of living. It was to His glory (which is another way of saying that He loves it), and He has been doing it for a long time.

The apostle Paul had his own cathartic event, after which he knew that God had chosen him and called him by His grace, and he knew that "God...was pleased to reveal His Son in me so that I might preach him among the Gentiles" (Galatians 1:15). Note Paul's exhortation to the Corinthians:

> So from now on we regard no one from a worldly point of view. Though we once regarded Christ in this way, we do so no longer. Therefore, if anyone is in Christ, he is a new creation; the old has gone, the new has come! All this is from God, who reconciled us to himself through Christ *and gave us the ministry of reconciliation*: that God was reconciling the world to himself in Christ, not counting men's sins against them. And he has committed to us the message of reconciliation. We are therefore Christ's ambassadors, as though God were making his appeal through us. We implore you on Christ's behalf: Be reconciled to God. God made him who had no sin to be sin for us, so that in him we might become the righteousness of God (2 Corinthians 5:16-21).

"The ministry of reconciliation" means that, all by Himself, God has done everything needed for a perfect family reunion. Through the cross and resurrection, our sin and failure and ugliness and weakness and resistance to God doesn't matter—the party has started, and our place is secured. The ministry or message of reconciliation is both the proclamation of that fact ("You can come in now!") and the insistence of our fit ("You belong!"). You're family! To some people, the message is an appeal to come for the first time. We, the church, are ambassadors of that incredible message in a land of foreigners, a worldwide arena of those who have not yet received Christ and are not yet family. *Come on in!* But to others—to those already reconciled and part of the party already—our message is an ongoing insistence that we're family and have no reason to hide. Not anything. Not ever. We're in. *We belong.*

Please don't cover up and project. You'll be acting dead.

The Ministry of Reconciliation

Let's pretend you're at a Friday night party of the reconciled. Imagine seeing a family member, a radiant and perfect son or daughter, skulking and miserable off to the side. What would you do? Would you tell him to quit hiding and to stop putting a damper on the party? "Act like you're having fun, you party pooper!" Would you tell him to start behaving better? No. That would be crazy. Trumped up enthusiasm for the sake of the party isn't genuine. And so, knowing there are genuine reasons for enthusiasm, you'd begin to lovingly serve those reasons to your downcast family member. Through your ministry and God's grace, the family member would come free in the moment, stand upright and brilliant, and enjoy the party—reconciled.

Or, at the same party, imagine seeing a family member who is overacting in a role that is hyper-caring, hyper-happy, and hyper-wise all in the span of a single minute. She's so good at being a Christian that there's no room for anyone else to offer anything. She's identified and taken care of everyone's needs. "Stand back, everyone! God's anointed is here!" What would you do? Would you tell her to back off and let someone else have a moment? "Take a load off, Martha!" Would you get in her way, blocking her from the next patient by ministering to their needs before she can? No. Instead, you'd realize that she was compensating for some inner crusade she was on, and you'd comfort her by talking with her about how good and sure and able God is. Perhaps you would help her to begin a season of being a spectator in God's theater. (A whole lot of us don't know just how good a show it is.)

That's the ministry of the church to the church. "You're in! Relax. Look what God has done—your worries are over! And I'm going to help you believe it in every possible way. God is in you, and you're in Him, merged and everything. How incredible is that?"

If there were a Ministry Fun-O-Meter placed on my heart, this service to God's sons and daughters would move it the most and the highest. It's what my ministry is all about. In my view, if there were a Ministry *Most Needed* Meter, the ministry of reconciliation would be highest.

Satan targets this issue more than just about anything else. He has been effective, because many of us are not freely enjoying the party. We're not convinced we're in, we're not sure we belong, but nevertheless we project a lifestyle that says we are. Not convinced, we work at pretending, and that's where the cover-up begins.

If we think that we've been reconciled by God but have not been made holy and blameless, we'll focus on making it happen. Books, seminars, and sermons on "How to Be Holy" and "How to Live a Life of Integrity" will capture our attention. We'll join the throng of disillusioned partygoers and begin handing out prescriptions for holiness and integrity: "Stop drinking alcohol, keep your promises, start tithing, say nice things to people, start praying more, learn how to serve better, and you'll be holy and have integrity."

Do you see the trade? Reconciliation, a stunning and accomplished fact we desperately need to believe, has been lost to something else, something that can be measured and increased and maintained. Can you say *performance*? When it all fails to cure what ails us, we'll hide that fact and do our best to make it look like it has succeeded. We'll project.

Remember Satan's Goal

And the Accuser of the party people will have pushed us away from the gospel and into a performance that keeps us from the delight of the celebration even while we walk about the reunion in family perfection. Paul set the Colossian Christians straight on this:

> Once you were alienated from God and were enemies in your minds because of your evil behavior. But now he has reconciled you by Christ's physical body through death

to present you holy in his sight, without blemish and free
from accusation—if you continue in your faith, established and firm, *not moved from the hope held out in the
gospel.* This is the gospel that you heard and that has been
proclaimed to every creature under heaven, and of which
I, Paul, have become a servant (Colossians 1:21-23).

As we've seen, Satan's goal is to move the church away from the
gospel of reconciliation, to get us to believe that we have not been
made holy and without blemish, that we've not been reconciled. If
he can seduce us into believing anything less than the gospel (if he
can get us to believe, for example, that at our core we're 75 percent
holy and 53 percent without fault), then we, the people of the gospel, won't believe the good news. Instead, we'll believe that God's
gift of righteousness and holiness and redemption (and all the other
incredible gifts we've received through Christ) have either not been
given to us or have been sullied and perhaps taken from us. *Now
what do we do?* Moved away from the gospel, we will no longer be
free from accusation. We'll take a pounding ("You idiot! You're so
stupid!"), and it will hurt.

So to stop the pain, we'll cover up. We won't live by faith, and
we won't trust God. But because our days and lives go on, we'll turn
on our projection system. After all, now there's work to be done. In
a terribly twisted way, we'll believe that we have to earn what has
been and will always be a *gift.* Then we'll measure ourselves and others by how we're looking, and by now we're really getting ourselves
together now. *Really.*

This is the primary misery plaguing the church. We're horribly
cheated when we go for the image we can perform instead of the
revival of faith and grace that the church is to assist us with.

To see if you've been affected, I want to ask you a question: If
people knew that you sometimes got sloppily drunk, were in an affair,
were lately looking at pornography, or were about to have an abor-
tion, who would you be most afraid of meeting: a roomful of Christians from your church, or a room full of people you didn't know?

If you responded, "I'd be most afraid of a roomful of Christians," you have something in common with me and 90 percent of the people who have previously answered the question. Think for a moment what that means. The implications are devastating. We're a church that doesn't like or trust each other—not really. How can we have fellowship on the grand scale befitting the church if we don't know what we have in common?

Since God's revelation about my bent-arm cover-up, the most difficult people for me to be around have been Christians. Not rookie Christians and not those recently born anew, but some of the veteran and leader types, those who shepherd the flock. They often don't see the church for who it has already become in Christ (having been reconciled), so they work to make something of it, to push it somewhere, and to make something happen—a bigger church. That means the members have to know what to do, how to look, how to reach out, how to love, how to obey, how to fight, and how to win. *Win!*

But because these leaders don't know who they already are (new creations), the projection way of life remains, and their hearts are left bound up, blocked from view, and blocked from life. Their only hope is God and His reconcilers.

I think that's pictured for us in what Jesus did with Lazarus.

Lazarus the Mummy

Perhaps you remember the story. Jesus had allowed Lazarus to die despite the well-intentioned pleas of his sisters. Lazarus had been in the tomb for four days when Jesus arrived, and virtually everybody thought He was late on the scene. Nevertheless, despite the protests of family and friends, Jesus called Lazarus to life and out of the tomb. Beyond the miracle of the moment, here's where the story gets interesting. Lazarus was still entirely wrapped head to foot in the grave clothes, yet managed to somehow blindly penguin-waddle out of the tomb anyway. He could not see or free himself, yet there he stood—a mummy with an audience.

And then this: "Jesus said to them, 'Take off the grave clothes and let him go'" (John 11:44). Another of way of saying it is, "Unbind him and let him live."

I wonder how fast the fan club for Lazarus the mummy got to him. Did they run, or did they delay? We don't actually know, but I'll bet they approached with caution. Were they quick with mummy-cloth removal, or did they take it off gingerly? Lazarus had been dead for four days—were they concerned about the smell? Martha was. Might they have been worried about what they would find underneath? After all, Lazarus was likely naked, and Jesus had commanded them to strip him.

And what about Lazarus himself? How might he have felt? Did he know he had been dead? Could he have preferred the cover of the grave clothes? Just a little here and there? I wonder if the sudden focus on Lazarus made him nervous. How would life be different from that day on?

One thing I know is that if those who loved him hadn't removed the grave clothes, Lazarus would have soon become enormously frustrated. He'd feel trapped. He'd feel as if he wasn't getting everything he should out of life. If friends and family had not unbound him, I imagine that before long he would have grown tired of trying to walk and simply given up the whole thing. "I'm not sure what's going on, but I quit!"

This is what happens if the church struggles in its ministry of reconciliation or fails to do it altogether. If we don't help convince new believers who they now are, and if we don't prove to them that they may walk among us without fear, safe and welcome because they're actually part of us, then we've left them in the tangle of their grave clothes. If we don't strip the mummies—and keep them stripped because they cannot go back to being dead—we all end up doing the penguin walk. We might even call it normal. Even as we tell everyone in Christ to run because they're free, no one really will be. Everyone will be impaired because everyone will be stumbling over the grave clothes we've not removed. The only place an unbound

Lazarus could fit in and not draw attention would be back in the tomb—as good as dead.

And we wonder why church is mostly boring. We're not truly impressed, and we're not actually engaged with one another. Imagine a sanctuary filled with mummies, and you've about got the picture.

This is what happens to believers when they're still wearing their own grave clothes. It doesn't matter whether they're new or long-time Christians. When they're not relieved of living as they once did because they've been made new, they cannot help "falling away" or "backsliding."

How Do We Address This Problem?

Three things have to happen in order for the newly alive to go free and live:

1. They have to know that the way they were before being born again is dead. Picture for them something out of a zombie film, and you've helped them.

2. They have to know that to live at all the way they once did is impossible. With God now living inside, the way forward is all new and different.

3. They have to know that you'll help them live in the freedom and safety and confidence of their new identity. You'll remind them of the gospel, and you'll help see to it that they're not pushed away from the truth and that there will never again be a moment of condemnation. That's how life works outside the tomb.

So how do we minister reconciliation? *Carefully.* Let me give you an example from my own life.

After God's revelation that He loved me regardless of my condition, experience, or behavior, I grew in the knowledge that I had been made new and well-off with Him. I loved being with God and knowing His thoughts and delight about me—the real me, the one made holy and blameless and without fault. I soon preferred Him to anyone else! He was incredibly faithful, even persistent to tell me and show me who He had made me to be. But I had no idea what that meant to anyone else.

Why should they think anything different of me? After all, I still looked the same. And, oh, what a problem that was. It seemed that the only way they would know I had been changed by God was if I performed better. If my behavior improved, if my prayer life grew deeper and longer in duration, if I led people in the sinner's prayer, if I faithfully attended church and brought people with me, if I tithed and read the right Bible translation, and if I stopped drinking alcohol and listening to rock and roll, *they would consider me changed.* "Hey! Ralph has finally changed! What do you know about that?"

With few exceptions, people told me to change, but they didn't help me believe *I had been changed.* They got it backward! They helped me to walk more acceptably and with a pleasing testimony, but they didn't help me to walk newly, as though I had just learned to walk for the first time or had died as one thing and been raised as another. Except for one or two friends, no one helped me walk away from my past dead way of living. I continued to cover up and project, but now I was covering the glory of God and blocking His work.

I had long been afraid of people anyway, so what do you suppose the odds were that I would now openly enjoy my new awareness of who I was? That I would stop blocking my heart and projecting an image? How do you think my audience would react if, during one night's performance, I broke with long-practiced and accepted protocol and proclaimed, "Hey, I am a blameless man, holy and faultless, a perfect son of God, recognized throughout the heavens"? What if you had been there with me? What would you have done? If your reaction would have included laughter and maybe ridicule ("Yeah, right…that's not the Ralph *I know*"), then you might understand if I turned coward and never did it again. And just how common do you suppose your response—laughter and ridicule—would be among others?

However, my cowardice didn't change the bit of pain God had in store for me.

The ministry of reconciliation will inescapably lead us into the sufferings of Jesus. If you'd rather not know about this part of it (thinking that ignorance might just be bliss), then jump ahead to the next chapter. Ignorance is, in fact, not bliss, but if for now you want to block your heart and happily project, "Gotta go somewhere," I'll understand. You won't escape God's intentions for you, but I'll understand.

Authentic Sons of the Light

Maybe 20 years ago, when I was fairly new at living without the cover-up, I led a men's retreat at a mountain cabin. For several days prior to the retreat, I hadn't been sleeping well, so I was very fatigued. One morning, I woke to find that all 18 of the men were already awake and downstairs. Shocked that I had slept soundly, I quickly got up and made my way to the stairs. Before I got ten feet, the sarcasm began. "Think you can sleep in because you're the leader, huh?" "What a lazy loser!" "Man! If I sacked out like that on my job, I'd be fired!" "All those in favor of firing Ralph, say 'Aye!'" There was no stopping it. The definition of sarcasm is "the tearing of flesh," and no one needed to convince me of the accuracy of it. It hurt.

Because I needed to buy the elements for us all to have communion later that morning, I mumbled something about going to the market and took the nearest exit. In the safety of my mobile tomb, I told God how I felt. *Father, I'm a mess! And all I want to do is to hide from those guys. I'm hurt, and I don't like it.* I carried on like that for a little while, and then, feeling better and secure, I asked, *Lord, what should I do?*

This is what I heard Him say: *Why not tell them that you're hurt?*

My immediate reaction was to cower and cover up. *You want me to tell them that?* I asked. *But that could make it worse. They would know that they had gotten to me. They would know how to do it again too.* Nevertheless, I knew it was the way forward, and because I trusted God, I left my cave and walked back into the torture chamber. At least that's how it felt.

Do you suppose that God had granted the men a repentant heart and that they warmly welcomed me? No way. It wasn't how God was working. *He was working me*, and I was greeted as before. "Oh, he's back! You need a nap, Ralph? Ha, ha, ha!" Everyone joined in the sarcastic chorus all over again. It was how they were relating to each other. Feeling like every comment was a knife wound, I called them together in the meeting area. How would you guess the men looked as they settled in? How do you think the room felt? Most were smiling, and the room was charged with competitive electricity, as if we'd been playing a sport.

While my flesh screamed that I should cover up and fake my way through communion—it was the safe way to go—I chose the way of the Spirit. "Well, guys, I'm a mess. I love you, but I don't know how that works right now. I may be stupid, but I feel chewed up, and all I want to do is get outta here. I feel like I've got holes in me, and I'm leaking oil. I'm afraid that you're going to keep shooting at me too. I don't know how to go forward into that."

And as I got quiet, everything changed. One guy said, "I hate that we do this. I'm just glad that it happened to you and not me."

"Me too," said another, "and I'm sorry. I got carried away and tore you up, even though I hate it when it happens to me."

"I don't really want to treat you this way, not when I love you and know who you are," said a friend.

The feeling in the room was completely different than it had been mere seconds before. It wasn't just that we were becoming emotional or vulnerable, even though we were. It was that we were beginning to prefer the reality of our life in Christ. My trust in God and willingness to go among them unbound and unprotected was the handle to the doorway of holiness. We could feel our view change from flesh to Spirit, and the difference was amazing.

Paul wrote to the church at Rome, "The mind set on the flesh is death, but the mind set on the Spirit is life and peace, because the mind set on the flesh is hostile toward God" (Romans 8:6-7 NASB).

As the men shifted their view from the flesh ("Ralph's a lazy bum!") to the Spirit ("Ralph's a son of God, and so are we"), we felt life and peace crowding out death and hostility. *We felt God*, and were unveiled and unencumbered before each other, without fear and free. Immediately, we loved! We beheld each other according to what God knew, and we were amazed! The light of it drove out the darkness and shadows that we had previously noted about each other. No longer did we major on minors. It didn't matter that we disagreed about what team or which politician was best. It didn't matter what car we drove or cell phone we had, and it didn't matter what fleshly or sinful hang-ups hounded us. We saw something tremendous—*reality!*—and it dwarfed all things lesser. Shockingly, it drained the power out of them as well.

We had suddenly revealed to ourselves that we were the sons of light. Fellowship was instant and authentic. It was something we knew, not just something we chose. In the freedom and love we shared, when we confessed fear, lust, covetousness, envy, drunkenness, and rage, it *was easy*. It was the natural thing to do. It was like picking leeches and ticks off one another—those parasites had no place with us! They were unsightly blemishes on the glory of God given to His sons. We could see sin as the ugly and unnatural rot it was, and men are notoriously good at fixing things. In the incredible light of what we knew, we calmly and gently took care of the rot that plagued us. Many times I heard someone happily say, "I'm so glad to be rid of that." We knew that freedom was now normal for each of us, and we served it to one another. Filled with vision, love, and hope, reconciliation became our new determination.

Centuries ago, Paul identified what we found:

> But you, brothers, are not in darkness so that this day should surprise you like a thief. *You are all sons of the light and sons of the day.* We do not belong to the night or to the

darkness. So then, let us not be like others, who are asleep, but let us be alert and self-controlled. For those who sleep, sleep at night, and those who get drunk, get drunk at night. But since we belong to the day, let us be *self-controlled*, putting on faith and love as a breastplate, and the hope of salvation as a helmet. For God did not appoint us to suffer wrath but to receive salvation through our Lord Jesus Christ. He died for us so that, whether we are awake or asleep, we may live together with him. Therefore encourage one another and build each other up, just as in fact you are doing (1 Thessalonians 5:4-11).

We knew who we were—"sons of the light and sons of the day"—so self-control was no longer a scary and valiant pledge of obedience to do something difficult. "I promise to be good, God!" Self-control meant living in keeping with who we had become—actual Spirit-born sons of God. And it meant living like that with everyone else who had also been made new and free. But when we're not impressed with who we are, self-control feels like a fight to become something we're not yet, like a bad person having to become a good person, an impossible work we have to create. Instead, we are each a work already done.

Knowing You're Reconciled Makes Confession Easy

When we know we've been reconciled to God, brought to life and led out of the tomb of our death, repentance and confession of sin became what they are for Christians—the awakening of faith that Christ has done everything for us and made us new, as well as a return to confidence in Him. When you and I grow weary or frustrated in the guaranteed failure of living after the flesh, we will eventually realize that living by the Spirit and in agreement with Him is the way for us now. The dawn of that realization leads to a change in how we go forward and often a declaration of what went wrong. *Jesus, I was tangled up with the flesh and seduced into the attempt to live like I used to when I was dead. I got fooled into living against myself,*

the self You've made, and sin was the result. I'm so glad You're not mad
at me and have been working to revive me. And I'm thankful for repen-
tance away from that crazy routine.

If you don't know that you've been reconciled to God, and if
you've not experienced being reconciled to other believers, then it's
likely that open repentance and confession of sin feels as though
you're forcing yourself to willingly take punishment. It might feel as
if you're getting into a line at church where you're going to be swat-
ted and served a terrible-tasting elixir by someone with a stern look
on his face. It's a horrible experience that everyone has, but it's appar-
ently needful if you're going to get right with God. And everyone
watching you will keep on watching you—examining your commitment. Entire churches get along like this.

But that's not what we found. Neither is it what the apostle
James found.

> Is any one of you in trouble? He should pray. Is anyone
> happy? Let him sing songs of praise. Is any one of you
> sick? He should call the elders of the church to pray over
> him and anoint him with oil in the name of the Lord.
> And the prayer offered in faith will make the sick per-
> son well; the Lord will raise him up. If he has sinned, he
> will be forgiven. Therefore confess your sins to each other
> and pray for each other so that you may be healed. The
> prayer of a righteous man is powerful and effective (James
> 5:13-16).

In that mountain cabin, we saw one another, righteous men
alive in faith in God, and we offered our prayers for each other. We
didn't worry about *who had the power* or *where the anointing was.*
We believed, we were convinced and relaxed, and God did what
He does when men dwell together in unity. We were alive and free
in the grace of God. We were living unbound together. Truly, the
sequence and meaning of Paul's words to the Colossian Christians
came alive in us.

Since, then, you have been raised with Christ, set your hearts on things above, where Christ is seated at the right hand of God. Set your minds on things above, not on earthly things. For you died, and your life is now hidden with Christ in God. When Christ, who is your life, appears, then you also will appear with him in glory.

Put to death, therefore, whatever belongs to your earthly nature: sexual immorality, impurity, lust, evil desires and greed, which is idolatry. Because of these, the wrath of God is coming. You used to walk in these ways, in the life you once lived. But now you must rid yourselves of all such things as these: anger, rage, malice, slander, and filthy language from your lips. Do not lie to each other, since you have taken off your old self with its practices and have put on the new self, which is being renewed in knowledge in the image of its Creator. Here there is no Greek or Jew, circumcised or uncircumcised, barbarian, Scythian, slave or free, but Christ is all, and is in all.

Therefore, as God's chosen people, holy and dearly loved, clothe yourselves with compassion, kindness, humility, gentleness and patience. Bear with each other and forgive whatever grievances you may have against one another. Forgive as the Lord forgave you. And over all these virtues put on love, which binds them all together in perfect unity.

Let the peace of Christ rule in your hearts, since as members of one body you were called to peace. And be thankful. Let the word of Christ dwell in you richly as you teach and admonish one another with all wisdom, and as you sing psalms, hymns and spiritual songs with gratitude in your hearts to God. And whatever you do, whether in word or deed, do it all in the name of the Lord Jesus, giving thanks to God the Father through him (Colossians 3:1-17).

I know that's a lengthy passage of Scripture, but do you see the order? It goes like this: When we know we've been reconciled to

God, we will become enamored with Him and how we are with Him and with each other. Looking at Him will reveal and renew us—*the real us*—and we'll say goodbye to the things of the flesh and the way we lived when we were dead. Living in the light of the new day, our new clothing of compassion, kindness, humility, gentleness, and patience will fit just right, and forgiveness will be our common language. And that's what love looks like—it's the evidence of Christ in us. Peace and the "word of Christ"—the sharing of who and what He is for us—will induce us to unending gratitude. That's what we found, and that's what happened for us in the mountains.

We Didn't Earn What We Found

We didn't earn what we found, and we didn't pray for it. In our simple humility and trust, God granted us the grace of life outside the tomb, life unencumbered by the grave clothes of our past.

No one wanted that weekend to end. But because we knew it would anyway, we left the mountaintop, delighted by what we had discovered, and we determined to grow in it in the valley. It wasn't easy.

The valley meant life as it had been. It meant a return to spouses, siblings, friends, classmates, employers, traffic, and the checkout line at the supermarket—each one an involvement with someone who saw and interacted with us. All of the people in our day-to-day lives knew us *before* the mountaintop unveiling, and they were ready for interaction based on what *had been*. However, we knew something they didn't, and that meant conflict. It also meant *growth*.

Telling someone you've known for a long time that you're holy, blameless, and without fault, and that God is as happy as He can be with you, is not often met with ready acceptance. Most of the men were not greeted with, "I knew it! I always suspected that you were perfect!" after telling a family member or friend the truth. To them, it sounded like a cop-out, a royal excuse, and a kingly demand for future acceptance and submission. We couldn't blame them. We hadn't been acting perfectly, so we couldn't expect them to share in our gleeful exuberance. But if we traded our biblical assessment for their unbiblical one, we would soon be floundering in doubt.

For most of us, that's how it went—floundering—at least at first. Some of us were seemingly swallowed up in the familiar feeling of living as we had before, just as if we were plugging back into the Matrix. But before long, we began to groan under the load of deception. Listening to lies about yourself (whether from the mouths of others or from the mouth of your flesh) is no fun, and we ached to again believe and be free.

We realized that if we were going to remain convinced about God and ourselves, if we were going to continue in "the grace of God that…teaches us to say 'No' to ungodliness and worldly passions, and to live self-controlled, upright and godly lives in this present age" (Titus 2:12), then we were going to have do everything we could to keep believing, and we were going to have to embrace our role as reconcilers. Not only was it the ministry given to us by God, but it was the only way we could help others and ourselves at the same time.

We had to build ourselves up and keep ourselves in the love of God (Jude 20-21), and we had to assist others toward reconciliation. From that time to this, many of us continue to pray for each other, call each other, and encourage each other in our true identity. We buy helpful books for each other. (For a sample, click on "Recommends" at the top of the page on my ministry website, www.Life Course.org.) We feed each other the grace and goodness of God. The apostle Paul encouraged his brothers in the faith toward this particular pattern of stability and vitality, and we've found it indispensible.

> Summing it all up, friends, I'd say you'll do best by filling your minds and meditating on things true, noble, reputable, authentic, compelling, gracious—the best, not the worst; the beautiful, not the ugly; things to praise, not things to curse. Put into practice what you learned from

me, what you heard and saw and realized. Do that, and
God, who makes everything work together, will work you
into his most excellent harmonies (Philippians 4:8-9 MSG).

The incredible harmonies we found during our weekend together
made us search for still more, and that meant we were living by
faith as we went among people. We wanted for them what we had
found—reconciliation. So we got along great with the gospel and
served it up to Christians and to those not yet. We didn't think of
ourselves as evangelists, nor did we think we were particularly bold.
We were working to wake the dead and to become friends with
them. It seemed natural.

A Christian in Hiding

As you would suppose, meeting and assisting people in need of
reconciliation is now one of the most common things in my day.
It's what I do.

Several years ago, I met Steve, who had been terribly disappointed
and hurt by someone he loved and trusted early in life. To say that
he didn't like it when people hurt him or took advantage of him is an
understatement, so he began to build defenses. It became his most
important work. His practice was to "play" in his mind a Simon and
Garfunkel song—"I Am a Rock"—over and over again. One might
think the song is a something of a curse, describing as it does a person who hides in an imaginary fortress behind self-erected walls, far
removed from the possibility of friendships and love for fear of the
pain that such things were sure to cause.

Steve estimates that song was at the top of the charts in his head
for years and that he played it thousands of times. It was his anthem,
his sacred song. He used it to keep anyone from knowing that he
was in pain. He might as well have had the words *I'm fine—stay
away* etched on his face.

In high school, the miraculous happened, and Steve became a
Christian. Strangely enough, much of what he began to learn fit

right in with what he already knew—*I don't like pain, so I'm hiding*—
and his newfound faith gave him hope of still more protection.

He learned how to project a happy attitude as a way of pleasing people and of keeping them from digging into his troubles. He
learned how to appear wise by holding his opinion until he could
come up with the perfect thing to say. People would be impressed
and leave him alone. He learned how to dress the right way, carry
the right Bible, pray the best way, and attend the proper events in
order to look healthy and stable. He learned that he could now hide
a little better. It was as if he had struck gold in the tomb.

Reaching the Breaking Point

For years, this was his chosen method. But creation is waiting "in
eager expectation for the sons of God to be revealed" (Romans 8:19),
so the smelly and filthy rags draped on a royal child of God must
one day be removed. Indeed, hiding in the techniques of a dead life
in order to protect ourselves will eventually bother us so much that
we'll ache to be free of them. We'll despise the methods, and we'll
hate the masks we wear in order to pretend we're experiencing something we're not. We'll loathe our projection ("I'm fine—stay away"),
and we'll search for ways to fall down in weariness. Many leave
church because they can no longer perform. Some will penguin-
waddle their way into an affair, the faux pleasure of pornography, or
the temporary fix of alcohol or drugs—all attempts at satisfying the
itch we cannot reach as long as the grave clothes cling to us.

In time, Steve could no longer play the game, so he left church.
At the same time, his wife began finding resources (books such as
Steve McVey's *Grace Walk*) and people (me) who showed her God's
opinion of her—and of her husband. She and I began to meet
weekly at a Dairy Queen, a safe and nonthreatening place. Over
various sugary delights, we talked about and worked through whom
we had become, thanks to God's gift of life-changing grace. When
Janet finally came out of the tomb of her past way of living, she was
like a lamb running out of a barn it has been shut up in all winter.

She'd say, "Are you sure? Is life with God really this good and secure? I'm not sure I can dare to hope again…but, my goodness, I do!" She was radiant. And why not?

Sometime later, urged on by his wife, Steve began peeking out from the tomb and into the light Janet was raving about. As any abused and intelligent Christian would, he kept his distance, like a lamb from a lion. While blocking his heart of lamblike feelings by projecting the confidence of a lion, Steve began to join our home church. Every time we get together at our church, we'll find a way to talk about the goodness of God to us in Christ, so he started hearing God's call to life outside the tomb. But it was quite a while before he responded to His call to come out.

God began convincing Steve about whom he had become—a holy and blameless child of God. It's commonly the first thing God does with His disbelieving children. But since it was someone loved and trusted who had hurt Steve many years ago, do you suppose God is taking His time with Steve? Of course He is. And think of the pleasure God gets in His work! Think of the glory God gets as Steve learns to trust in God's assessment over and against what his flesh has trained him to believe and follow. I imagine that heaven has danced with glee each time Steve has allowed God to get close, to hold, console, and reassure him—and to call him out of the tomb.

And that's where we come in.

Our ministry of reconciliation to Steve is careful, gentle, and persistent. We know who he is, so when he doubts or falters, we're there to encourage and remind him of what God thinks. Sometimes we get to watch as trust in God is restored to Steve. That's a beautiful thing to witness. More than once, I've noticed extra water in his eyes, but I'm not about to announce it to our group: "Hey! Look at Steve, everyone! God's finally getting to him! Well, hallelujah!" In light of how truly sacred this all is and of how capable God is, no one's in a hurry. Steve is growing.

Janet wants to be forever out of the tomb and to be rid of the grave clothes of her past. She doesn't want anything to do with what

204 GOD'S ASTOUNDING OPINION OF YOU

once was. She hates what she was and did when she used to be dead. The ministry of reconciliation seems comparatively easy with her. Tell Janet that God is just a little bit nuts about her, and she'll beam like a 17-year-old just asked out by her dream date. On the other hand, Steve has thought for a long time that his grave clothes were the only way of securing himself against pain. You trust someone, you let them get close, and they hurt you. Just think of the damage All-knowing, almighty God could do if you let Him get close. *Danger!* Do you see the difficulty? The lifestyle of blockading and projecting seems almost reasonable when you've been hurt. Everyone's past is different, as is their way out of the tomb, so we offer ourselves to God and submit to each other in order to walk faithfully together.

The ministry of Christian reconciliation, the delightful task of telling Christians that they are right now in perfect union with God, happens in lots of ways and by various means. Let me tell you about a couple of other times I've watched this ministry occur.

Sowing to the Spirit Can Lead to Reconciliation

On most days during my conversations with God, I say something about how I want to be open and not barricaded before people so they can get whatever they need from God. I talk with people a lot, whether in person or by phone, Internet video, Facebook, or e-mail, so I want to be aware of God and what He wants for those people and situations. I don't want to *act* as if I'm open and concerned for people—I want to *know* that I am. So I talk with Dad about it, and He is really good with me.

On a restful Saturday morning, several of us were talking about what God has done for us through Jesus' death and resurrection. Some were receptive and talkative, but one or two others were stone-faced and silent. After answering a question, I focused on one stone-faced young lady. Why? Because the Spirit brought my attention and concentration to her. I knew something was coming. Looking into her eyes, I said this to Cindy: "You must know that God finds

no fault with you—not one. He is delighted with you, His magnificent daughter, and He will always see to your cares and fears. He is
not at all mad at you for worrying about your future. He knows it's
a mystery. So He will hold you in the wonder and dispel fear. He
chose you and will never forsake you."

She gasped, her eyes flew open, and out poured tears. Everyone
in the room knew something beautiful and intimate was happening, and joy and peace filled us. We knew that God was rescuing her
from something damaging. When Cindy could speak, she told us
that fear had been her constant companion for many years. Com-
pounding her struggle, she had been taught that worry was sinful
and that she shouldn't and couldn't and better not have anything
to do with it—*or else.* The only thing to do, then, was to go on a
personal crusade against fear, which resulted in an inner offensive
against herself. Or so she believed.

But that Saturday, God once again moved her back to the gospel—"I have made you faultless, and I am with you!"—and, free
from the accusations that had been plaguing her, she was reconciled. We marveled.

When I asked her how she felt as I spoke a message of reconciliation to her, Cindy told us that she was initially nervous. She said,
"It felt like you were looking inside me and talking to me from there.
I've never experienced anything like it, and at first, I wanted to hide.
But then I realized that God was doing something wonderful with
me, and I wanted that more than I wanted to hide. And now I feel
light, as if something heavy has been lifted from me. I feel great!"

Some people in the room said that they were aware of how deeply
personal it was and that they were also a little nervous at first. One
person said she was concerned that Cindy might be hurt because
we had broken through her defenses. "You mean the way I fake you
into believing I'm okay?" Cindy asked. "You did go past that, but
I'm so glad! I'm not scared of you anymore! A little while ago I was,
but not now. I'm okay—no, I'm great!"

Can you imagine how good that was for Cindy and for us? That's the church—a community (no matter how small) of believers who, without fear, walk together openly in God-given radiance. Cindy was set free that day, and a gang of reconcilers was born.

That's what I want for the whole church. Can you imagine it? I hope so.

Looking Past the Grave Clothes

At a weekend seminar a couple of years ago, I was teaching about our identity as new-creation sons and daughters of God. Frankly, people were really enjoying the biblical discovery, so after a break, I decided to go further with the group. I silently asked God if He wanted to impress someone in the room, someone who would benefit from a helpful unveiling. The face of one of the men came to mind, so I asked if he would be okay with standing alongside me. When he arrived, I asked the group if they knew him very well. They assured me they did. So I gave them the following scenario: "Let's say that I am meeting this fellow for the first time, and you're introducing him to me. Help me get to know Roger (not his real name) by telling me what he's like. You know, cut down my learning curve." Well, his friends called out lots of things about Roger. "He's funny." "He's a perfectionist." "He likes hockey."

At that point, I thanked them for their help, and then I said, "Okay. Now I'd like you to tell Roger—don't tell me, tell Roger—who God thinks he is. Tell Roger what kind of man God knows him to be. Take your time with this. Think about it."

In the quiet of the next moment, we could feel a tremendous change take place in the room. One moment we were a raucous gang of laugh-it-up buddies, and the next we were the holy ones of God, pointing out the sacredness of our friend. "You're a blameless man," said one. "God lives in you," said another breathlessly. "You're holy already," said a woman, whose hands were pressed against her cheeks in sudden wonder. "The angels recognize you. You're family," murmured another, "and they praise God because of you."

And from someone in the back, "You totally bug the devil!"

With tears in our eyes, we laughed loudly and freely, and someone added, "It's true! You're a son of God, and you're a threat to Satan."

No one had ever seen him like this—not until we really looked—not until we looked past the grave clothes to the man within.

Interestingly, Roger didn't like it. After asking him what he felt, Roger told us that we were wrong about him. Even though we'd spent a day and a half discussing together our new identity in Christ, Roger wasn't convinced it was true. I think we all felt a bit like fish trying to swim away when there is no water. But we held together. "This must be very awkward for you," I said, "and I'm sorry for that." A longtime friend of Roger's said, "But Roger, I've always thought of you this way. You're brilliant! Your actions, as far as I know, have always been great and godly. I wouldn't have thought that you would be troubled with this. Why?"

And then it happened—off came Roger's grave clothes. "Look! I've been acting all good and holy for years, but it's a fake! I'm not! I struggle with so many things, but I'm able to pull myself together and fool you. I'm a fake. I'm not holy, I'm not blameless, and I doubt that I ever bug the devil."

We were silent…and awkward. And then someone said, "Well, I'm so glad to hear that. I love you! More now than ever before. In fact, I used to act around you too! You were so good that I put on goodness to match yours. And now I don't have to! We can be together—fakers for God! Anybody want to join us?" Every hand in the room went up.

We were free. We were wonderful. And none of us were trying to be. Invisible facades laying about the room, we came out of hiding and pretending, and we found God together.

Like most of us, Roger had been living after the flesh. It seemed logical to him. And why wouldn't it? Our flesh can seem like a faithful assistant on the way to the fruit of the Spirit or against the behavior of the flesh. And when we are deceived into the attempt to live by it, making the suggested right moves and decisions on our way to the goal, not only are we set up for failure, we're set up to hide. Living after the flesh means that we believe we are supposed to muster sufficient resources and make the right choices to change ourselves and "do the right thing." As we've seen, failure is the guaranteed result. And because we have worked so hard and employed our best wisdom, we cannot help but go into a sort of invisible seclusion, a secret place inside where personal accountability means personal punishment—we'll isolate ourselves, even at a party.

Turn on the projection system.

If we don't know that we're not the flesh, and if we don't have a small group of people who know we're not the flesh, then living free of the grave clothes of your past will be terribly difficult. It won't take much to induce us to return to the tomb.

An Archaeological Discovery

Let's pretend that an ancient text of Exodus 20:15 is found under a rock in the Sinai Desert. It is discovered that, shockingly, the eighth commandment, "You shall not steal," actually means, "You shall not take a cephalopod into the local library." Word soon spreads around the globe about the change in meaning, and libraries are put on alert. How long before naughty teens begin sneaking squid and saltwater aquariums into their basements? Can you imagine a sudden buying spree on sea salt and brine shrimp? And what kind of detection system would security guards use at the library door as they hunted for loaded Tupperware? I suspect the police would have to get involved, don't you? And think of the shame brought on families when once a squid smuggler was caught and jailed. The only safe place for those addicted to squid smuggling would be at a small group meeting of those with similar struggles. "Hi. My name is Bob, and I haven't smuggled an octopus into my local library for 13 months and 4 days." Hooray for Bob!

Do you see what's happened? There's no way for Bob to believe that he has been reconciled to God unless he stays away from slimy creatures without bones. Just try telling him—as he hangs his head in shame for thinking again of buying some more squid—that he has already been reconciled, and watch his face. He won't believe you. But if you stay with him and love him, reassuring him that you're for him, even while he's scheming about getting cephalopods into libraries, you might take away his fear of hiding, at least with you. He could tell you how awful he thinks he is. He could wail in anguish about his inability to stop, even though his family is suffering because of it. He could come out of hiding with you, and that will make you the most important friend Bob has.

You'll be like Jesus to him.

That's what reconcilers are—people who, without a hint of condemnation, rescue men and women, boys and girls who are being tormented and corrupted by the flesh, and who are covering up and hiding. Wouldn't it be great to have a whole church full? That's what Jude envisioned.

> But you, dear friends, build yourselves up in your most holy faith and pray in the Holy Spirit. Keep yourselves in God's love as you wait for the mercy of our Lord Jesus Christ to bring you to eternal life. Be merciful to those who doubt; snatch others from the fire and save them; to others show mercy, mixed with fear—hating even the clothing stained by corrupted flesh. To him who is able to keep you from falling and to present you before his glorious presence without fault and with great joy—to the only God our Savior be glory, majesty, power and authority, through Jesus Christ our Lord, before all ages, now and forevermore! Amen (Jude 20-25).

This is what we do! But consider this scenario: What if, instead of encouraging and reassuring Bob about what God thinks of him, his friend Bill shows up and shames him? "Your clothing reeks of squid, you promise-breaking smuggler! God is so disappointed with you. You'd better repent because you don't know what tomorrow may bring—I'm telling you!" Bob would go into hiding, even while going through the motions of repentance and rededication to stop squid smuggling. He'd take another stand for God, and both fear and failure would plague him.

Coming Out of Hiding

Christians waging secret war against the flesh have no chance of winning—and they hate themselves for it. However, Christians with trusted friends around them, who know and share in the battle to live by the Spirit while hounded by the flesh, will grow together as the body of Christ, with gifts and grace abounding. They might even laugh together at the crude and rude temptations of the flesh and the devil: "Anybody else have flesh that thinks sneaking squid into a library is the most fun thing in the world? You too, Ralph? Isn't that the craziest evidence that it is much better to live by the Spirit than by the flesh? I know that fight well, and I'll help you in yours. I know what it's like to return to the stained grave clothes of how I used to live by corrupt flesh."

Bob and Ralph then help each other not to cover up, and they walk by the Spirit so that they won't join the worldly play of pretending to be doing well even when experience proves otherwise. Together, they're free from the lunatic effort of parading their own righteousness by sprucing up their wardrobe and attitude. They don't have to hide. If the grace of God means anything, it's this: In light of what God thinks He has done *for* and *to* us through Christ, we walk together in humility without competition, condemnation, or cover-ups produced by shame. Trusting God together with ourselves—who we are, what we've done, and what we'll be—means a love affair, grand and reckless. It's like leaving a dark cave of isolation for the freedom of sunlight. It's risky! But it's living. This kind of relationship is how our godly character is formed—by serving and assisting others. When our truest selves are truly accepted, loved, and needed, then we'll come out of hiding. It's not that we won't ever sin or drape ourselves with smelly and stained grave clothes all over again. We will. But knowing who we are, we won't let each other go back to the cave! We'll be after each other with love and care and maybe a pair of scissors (to remove those grave clothes). We'll trust ourselves to God and to each other—and God will be obvious. Isn't that what Christianity is about anyway?

We'll be like children! In this kind of community, there will be joy and laughter and stumbling and playfulness and support and worship and awe. And love! Loads and loads of love, both poured out and drunk in. In my opinion, a community that receives love is church. It means that we trust and know we're safe, and that we are no longer walking as mummies, covering up and projecting an image of goodness that once seemed to work in our past way of living.

Here's how The Message phrases Paul's passionate words to the Galatians about *real* living:

> We know very well that we are not set right with God by rule-keeping but only through personal faith in Jesus Christ. How do we know? We tried it—and we had the best system of rules the world has ever seen! Convinced that no human being can please God by self-improvement, we believed in Jesus as the Messiah so that we might be set right before God by trusting in the Messiah, not by trying to be good. Have some of you noticed that we are not yet perfect? (No great surprise, right?) And are you ready to make the accusation that since people like me, who go through Christ in order to get things right with God, aren't perfectly virtuous, Christ must therefore be an accessory to sin? The accusation is frivolous. If I was "trying to be good," I would be rebuilding the same old barn that I tore down. I would be acting as a charlatan (Galatians 2:15-18 MSG).

No more blocking our hearts. No more projecting an image. We've died to that, and for us, "to live is Christ" (Philippians 1:21).

Seeing Christians for Who They Are, Not How They Behave

As we've seen in previous chapters ("Cleaning Up Toxic Relationships," "The Eyes Have It," and "Aliens Have Landed"), when our Christian friends and family and even Christians we don't know appear before us, what we see is not what's real. Those who love being reconciled to God and believe it's the greatest thing there is will learn to approach people according to what they have become in Christ, not according to how they behave. It will be exhilarating for them. No, they won't do it all the time or every time they meet someone. That could become a new form of legalism: "How many Christians have I told about their identity in Christ today? Better reach my daily quota." But it will be a great way of building themselves up and living by faith. And they won't do it childishly or callously: "Hey! Look what we've got here, everybody—a special child of God! A sanctified saint! Wow! Let's give God a clap offering, okay?" That makes eternal and extraordinary truth ordinary and cheap. It would become too common to the speaker—a conversational lubricant—and of no affect to the hearer. If done very much, the hearers learn to ignore it.

Reconcilers will regularly enjoy a quick and healthy pause toward God, and they will receive from the Spirit the unveiled truth. It will affect them. Reconcilers will experience a lot of things, including being sobered and calmed by what the Spirit does, awakened by what they believe, and moved by what they know. They won't settle for looking or sounding like they're reconcilers. They won't playact. They'll crave the reality of it. That will keep them humble, genuine, sincere, and caring. Reconcilers are the most approachable and considerate people I know, and I want you to know a lot of them—maybe even become one.

You may begin.

Questions for Discussion

1. What does Ralph mean when he writes about "blockading and projecting"?

2. What does being "reconciled to God" mean to you? What does reconciliation tell you about others?

3. What would a gathering of reconcilers be like?

4. Would you like to be part of that bunch? Why?

Chapter Fifteen

Taking Heaven with You

If All of Heaven Is Your Audience, What Are They Thinking?

The kingdom of heaven is like treasure hidden in a field.
When a man found it, he hid it again, and then in his
joy went and sold all he had and bought that field.

MATTHEW 13:44

Heaven wheels above you, displaying to you her eternal
glories, and still your eyes are on the ground.

DANTE ALIGHIERI

When I was in grade school, I became increasingly aware of—and sometimes uncomfortable with—the fact that people had opinions about me. It all began when it was obvious that a girl *liked* me. Annalise approached my kingdom in the school sandbox during lunchtime with more in mind than a comment about my stately castle and moat. I think my layout had clarified for her what she wanted in life—*me*. "We're going to get married, and I'm going to buy you a watch and T-shirt," she proclaimed.

I stared at my castle. Annalise remained at my side, humming a pleasant tune in keeping with her romantic vision. Fortunately, the school bell rang, interrupting her blissful dream but providing a merciful escape for me. "Well, bye," I uttered.

I don't think I broke her heart, but I sure discovered something of my own.

Annalise woke me up. I suddenly noticed that my teacher liked me, and as my astute eight-year-old daughter once said, "I like people who like me." It made me feel good. And then there was Heidi. I thought she was the most beautiful third grader in the world, and that made me want her to think I was beautiful too. I remember how I felt when she did. What a validation it was—beauty recognizing beauty. It made my heart sing.

A Heavenly Chorus

Consider what you've found through the pages of this book and how you've felt as a result. In contrast to what you once thought about yourself, don't you now feel better off? Why? Because now you're looking in the right place. You've swapped this world's opinion of yourself for God's view, and it's changing your life. I hope you've found a new and holy craving to know God and are learning that it is a satisfying, wonderful labor of faith. His opinion of you is true and better by far than any you've ever known, and knowing it does something to you. If God, who is perfect beauty, affirms *you as beauty*, your life changes dramatically, and your heart sings! And it won't be a solo. Your song will join the adoring chorus of the heavenly choir now thundering their delight and awe of God.

> And they sang a new song: "You are worthy to take the scroll and to open its seals, because you were slain, and with your blood you purchased men for God from every tribe and language and people and nation. *You have made them to be a kingdom and priests to serve our God, and they will reign on the earth.*"
>
> Then I looked and heard the voice of many angels, numbering thousands upon thousands, and ten thousand times ten thousand. They encircled the throne and the living creatures and the elders. In a loud voice they sang: "Worthy is the Lamb, who was slain, to receive power and wealth and wisdom and strength and honor and glory and praise!"
>
> Then I heard every creature in heaven and on earth and under the earth and on the sea, and all that is in them,

singing: "To him who sits on the throne and to the Lamb be praise and honor and glory and power, for ever and ever!" (Revelation 5:9-13).

Heaven is singing! And why? Because of what God has made of you! Looking out over men and women and boys and girls who are made sons and daughters of God, all those in heaven are wild with ecstasy! They see the glory of God in the vessels of His grace, and they're singing with abandoned glee. They recognize beauty in us. This is heaven's view of you and me, and this is heaven's response to the One who made it so. The rest of your life will be about the growing confidence and grace you gain by accepting heaven's view as reality and living from it—made in His image and sharing in His glory. You were once a beast, and now you're a beauty, recognizing your own beauty. Incredible! Amazing!

I remember tossing my delighted and squealing daughters up into the air and catching them, only to hear them exclaim, "Do it again, Daddy! Do it again!" And I think the angels are saying something similar as they watch in wonder as God changes another person into a holy dwelling place for Himself. "Incredible! Do it again, Father! Do it again!"

The four living creatures, the 24 elders, and the thousands and thousands of angels gathered together in joyful adoration are celebrating Jesus and what He has done with you and me. They are jubilant because they see the astonishing goodness of God in His outrageous grace to us. They simply can't get over the display of God's generosity in vessels so inherently unworthy—what a thrill! "Incredible! Do it again!" The angels know what we must know. And the angels are focused where we must focus.

All those in heaven see earth as the stage for God, and those of the heavenlies never become so transfixed by what happens on the stage that they quit looking at the Conductor. They're fascinated with Him! The amazing creatures and angels only glance at you and me, but they stare at God, marveling at His grace. And that's where our gaze should go also. Rejoice over those whom God has made righteous and holy, but become transfixed by the One who made them that way. Looking to Him who is unseen, you will be convinced and refreshed by what is truly true!

Enjoying Ourselves in Christ

That's why we fix our thoughts and hearts on things above, in the heavens, and not on earthly things (Colossians 3:2). We don't do it so we'll feel better about ourselves and have a nice day. We do it because that's where we're made visible and where our desire for the Beautiful One who made us beautiful is satisfied. And we ought to be satisfied by Him again and again. We should seek our own satisfaction and delight in God—to be as happy as we can in Him. C.S. Lewis explains this vitally important truth this way:

> If there lurks in most modern minds the notion that to desire our own good and earnestly to hope for the enjoyment of it is a bad thing, I submit that this notion has crept in from Kant and the Stoics and is no part of the Christian faith. Indeed, if we consider the unblushing promises of reward and the staggering nature of the rewards promised in the Gospels, it would seem that our Lord finds our desires, not too strong, but too weak. We are half-hearted creatures, fooling about with drink and sex and ambition when infinite joy is offered us, like an ignorant child who wants to go on making mud pies in a slum because he cannot imagine what is meant by the offer of a holiday at the sea. We are far too easily pleased.*

"Delight yourself in the LORD" (Psalm 37:4) is not a command to dance about and make merry as though the appearance of delight fulfills the command. It's a directive for our own enjoyment! When we find God to be our greatest joy and pleasure, the presumed pleasures

---

* C.S. Lewis, "The Weight of Glory," *The Weight of Glory and Other Essays* (Grand Rapids, MI: Eerdmans, 1965), 1-2.

of drink and sex and ambition and covetousness are exposed as the empty pretenders they are, and their grip upon us is loosened.

When I discovered the crazy love and joy I received from communion with God, I began gladly trading the many worldly pleasures for the one. It took little calculation on my part because I had so much delight. No one needed to tell me that bar-hopping, drink-pounding, and women-chasing on Saturday night violated God's commands and must be stopped for the glory of God. I found that He is truly delightful and pleasurable to be with (just as He says), and Saturday night carousing ceased to be the fun it once was. Even a little of it was like skipping any stages of fun and going right to the hangover on Sunday morning! Besides, what glory is in it for God if the reason I cease Saturday night bingeing is not out of finding Him actually glorious and worthy and better but out of presumed duty?

I would not have discovered anything good about God except that He's a demanding killjoy, and there's no glory in that—neither is it true. And since God has wired me (and everyone) to seek and to find pleasure and satisfaction, when I don't find either after denying myself what little I had, I will come to resent Him and begin sinning again.

John Piper explains the difference between true worship and mere acts of duty:

> Worship is a way of gladly reflecting back to God the radiance of His worth. This cannot be done by mere acts of duty…Consider the analogy of a wedding anniversary. Mine is on December 21. Suppose on this day I bring home a dozen long-stemmed red roses for Noel. When she meets me at the door I hold out the roses, and she says, "O Johnny, they're beautiful, thank you," and gives me a big hug. Then suppose I hold up my hand and say matter-of-factly, "Don't mention it; it's my duty." What happens? Is not the exercise of duty a noble thing? Do not we honor those we dutifully serve? Not much. Not if there's no heart in it. *Dutiful roses are a contradiction in terms…*In fact they

belittle her. They are a very thin covering for the fact that she does not have the worth or beauty in my eyes to kindle affection. All I can muster is a calculated expression of marital duty.*

When and if we're reduced to empty-hearted displays of affection for God, we subtly begin believing that He likes the display even if we don't. And what often comes from that point is a detrimental style of living many call normal—the show of worship and obedience goes on, but our hearts are far off. In other words, we do things to please Him, but we remain unaware and without the benefit of knowing and sharing in His pleasure. And the distance grows from there, as does the lifestyle.

Redirecting Our Gaze

One day I was in one of those dreary funks where nothing was particularly bad or good, but I felt a bout of "zombieness" had come over me. Looking in the mirror, I saw a body with skin, hair, and eyes but seemingly without any blood or muscle to get the whole thing going. *What a stiff,* I thought. *Oh, well. I've got work to do.* As I turned to leave and launch into work, the Spirit interrupted the course of my thinking with two words: *Delight yourself.*

Now since God has proven Himself to be my treasure and greatest delight, I knew immediately that He was directing me toward a revival by enjoying God. I'll bet He has with you too. So His command to delight myself directed me to Him so that I could share in the perspective of heaven, which remains in glad awe of God. He is always on display there, and what He thinks and does drives everybody nuts with joy. Nobody there makes the attempt to be or look happy, nor do they concern themselves with their attitude—they look at Him, and that's sufficient!

Looking at myself in the mirror, I saw confirming evidence of

---

* John Piper, *Desiring God: Meditations of a Christian Hedonist* (Colorado Springs, CO: Multnomah Books, 1986), 72-73.

why I felt lifeless. Redirecting my gaze toward heaven's view did something about it. My flesh conspired against me to keep me visibly oriented, tempting me to sow toward it: "Man! I'll bet I've got zombie breath to match. Oh, well. I've got work to do." The flesh might have furthered the course by suggesting, "There's no time to seek God. Just be faithful to do the work at hand the best you can. God likes faithfulness." Following that course, I might have breathed out an empty-hearted prayer and remained in the weariness that had my attention. Fortunately, the Spirit broke up the conspiracy, redirected my perspective toward heaven's view, and wooed me back to the proper vision for a son of God. "O Father. What are Your thoughts today? What's happening with You?" I asked aloud. And in about ten seconds, I looked like heaven.

I had a revival in my bathroom. And it wasn't like I was given an injection lasting for only a few hours of strength. The cover this world puts over heaven was removed, and I could see again. I could see my Love! Living again by faith and filled with the Spirit, I went into the work of the day, taking heaven with me. *I could see clearly.*

Heaven is celebrating God's grace to us in Christ. Returning over and over again to heaven's view and focus is the most vital and invigorating workout you and I will undertake—it's worth everything! Celebrating God's grace to us is essentially this: *Father, we believe and are staggered by the fact that You have given us everything for nothing. And You always will. Incredible! Astounding! To You who sit on the throne and to the Lamb be praise and honor and glory and power, forever and ever!*

We can't get over it. And why should we? If God's grace and glory to us is the thrill of heaven, why shouldn't it be ours? It is! And finding virtually any way to remind yourself and others that He has given us *everything* for *nothing* is the way to the best of life and the best of you. It's how you live by faith.

As we saw in chapter 12, it isn't a list of do's and don'ts that teaches and equips us best toward righteous living, and neither is it an accountability group so your feet can be held to the fire. And no, it isn't forcing oneself to surrender and do the will of God. What makes for the best of life is looking upon the magnificence of God! That heavenly view stimulates faith, which is how we live—by faith. Any other manner trips up the Christian by dragging his or her focus from heaven's view and diverting it to an earthly one. And so the stumbling begins.

Those Stumbling Galatians

That's what happened to the Galatians. Even though they had been given everything for nothing and had received the Holy Spirit, the guarantor or underwriter of every promise, the Christians at Galatia were still losing focus and taking a different view. They were falling from wonder, and they were *falling from grace*.

Those who denied that Christians had been given everything for nothing in Christ had stealthily crept in to introduce old ways, former ways of securing God's favor. What turned Galatian heads was the lie that they didn't have His favor and blessing already in Christ but could have it if they would add to their faith a few practices— just a few rituals from the past. Then they would be even better off. Then God would really give them the grace and blessing and life they'd dreamed about.

Do you see the lie? Even though they were in Christ, new creations and children of God, these "bewitchers" suggested the Galatians' condition with God had not been made perfect: "Jesus' death on the cross was insufficient, and His resurrection only partially secured a new day and new covenant. Sure, Jesus did *most* of the work, but here's what remains. Do this and do that, He'll see you do it, and the blessings of heaven will be yours. Fail to do this and that and, well, you know what history shows—it won't be pretty. And just look at your behavior. You know you don't live as you should. You don't think God will bless you living the way you are, do you?"

In other words, look at yourself outside of Christ, take an earthly view, and get with it! Start doing what God requires so He won't cut you off from His blessings. And these wicked workers dragged the former covenant into the new, creating a twisted and unrecogniz-able monstrosity. How gruesome it is when a Christian attempts to live by the former covenant.

The apostle Paul was overwhelmed with grief and righteous anger at those who would rob God of His glory in Christ: "Does God give you his Spirit and work miracles among you because you observe the law, or because you believe what you heard?" (Galatians 3:5).

Wake up, Galatians! You've got everything for nothing simply because you believe in what Christ has done! You've accepted heav-en's view, and you're astonishingly well-off because of it. You're free from the fear of thinking that God determines His treatment of you based upon your ability to earn it. He has made you sons and daughters in perfect standing! Don't let those bewitchers make you into slaves by agreeing to their miserable principles—they're worse than useless! And have you noticed that your joy is missing? It's gone because you've forgotten God's opinion of you, and you've accepted the opinion of someone else. And now you're believing and follow-ing men who want you to do what *they* think is best. They may be motivating you, but they're making you into something tragic—sons and daughters of God who don't believe what their Father believes! *How can you go forward in Christ?*

Because the glory of God was at stake, that twist was driving Paul crazy.

> It is for freedom that Christ has set us free. *Stand firm,* then, and do not let yourselves be burdened again by a yoke of slavery.
>
> Mark my words! I, Paul, tell you that if you let yourselves be circumcised, *Christ will be of no value to you at all.* Again I declare to every man who lets himself be circumcised that he is obligated to obey the whole law. You who are trying to be justified by law have been alienated from Christ; *you have fallen away from grace.* But by faith we eagerly await through the Spirit the righteousness for which we hope.

> For in Christ Jesus neither circumcision nor uncircumcision has any value. The only thing that counts is faith expressing itself through love (Galatians 5:1-6).

By attempting to earn God's approval and favor (verse 4), the Galatian Christians had "been alienated from Christ" or *stuck in neutral*. No matter how diligently they worked, no matter how much they revved their motors and honked their horns, urged on by the bewitchers, they couldn't move. And out of anguished love, Paul was calling them to return to faith in Jesus. After all, they are so much better off with Him. Only that would secure them and give them confidence to approach God's throne of grace, expecting to receive what He had already earned! (See Hebrews 4:16.)

Would God actually "work miracles" simply because they believed? Shouldn't there be more to it? *No!* There isn't more. That's it! It's astounding—praise God! Everyone in heaven was praising Him for it, but the Galatians were chasing after the demonic lure of adding something lacking in order to earn the everything they had for nothing.

Has the devil dragged the Galatian lure by your nose lately? Because the Galatians bit on it, they suffered terribly, and so do we if we're fooled.

My brother, my sister, no matter how that lure comes, and no matter who throws it by you, quickly look away from it to heaven's view of things, and do not bite. Ignore the lie by preferring the truth. Wherever you go, take heaven's view with you—keep it close! As prevalent as the lie is today, that will take some doing.

Inactivity, an Enemy of Grace

Some people have a misunderstanding of what living by grace entails for the Christian. These believers may think that Christians who live by grace don't do anything but wait upon the motivational *push* of the Spirit. While perhaps fairly characterizing them as reluctant to live by any rules by which they might become *more* holy or *more* righteous, others fail to see what great efforts people who live by grace make every day.

The fact and effectiveness of God's grace to us in Christ does not mean we do not make real and serious choices about life and about what we do daily. To the contrary, God's grace means not only that we get to revel in Christ, finding ourselves animated because of His life within us, but also that *we choose* to revel in Christ. In truth, that choice becomes our single most important act of faith.

> So then, just as you received Christ Jesus as Lord, continue to live in him, rooted and built up in him, strengthened in the faith as you were taught, and overflowing with thankfulness. See to it that no one takes you captive through hollow and deceptive philosophy, which depends on human tradition and the basic principles of this world rather than on Christ. For in Christ all the fullness of the Deity lives in bodily form, and you have been given fullness in Christ, who is the head over every power and authority (Colossians 2:6-10).

If we are to have the grace of God at work within us, then aside from those marvelous times in which the Spirit sovereignly and surprisingly wells up within us toward some effect, we must do lots of things in keeping with the new life we now have, "stimulating" our true selves. *Inactivity* can easily become an enemy of grace.

If the believer just waits around for the Spirit's activity or motivation, kicking back and doing nothing with what he knows about the kingdom within him, then his problem isn't laziness—it's unbelief. Whether he has been overwhelmed or underwhelmed by the circumstances of life, unbelief has crept in and taken him captive. He's miserable because of it. The good news is that the Christian can have the best of life at any point by choosing to live in Christ. A reviving fullness greets us whenever we overcome creeping unbelief by remembering all we have been given in Him.

Sometimes when my efforts or hopes have taken a beating, and lethargy or disappointment threatens to seize me, I'll take a walk and verbalize all that is mine in Christ. As I talk aloud about having His righteousness and His holiness, I often realize I've begun to rely upon my own works as my righteousness and holiness—my own seal of approval. That will never do! So I make the choice to see myself *where I am* and *as I am*—in Christ, having all things. And that choice to give thanks restores Spirit-filled confidence and strength.

As a result of that choice, our delight in our status as sons and daughters of God will be evident in our lives. Worship will be genuine, service a joy, humility natural, friendship sincere, giving heartfelt, and caring authentic.

Living by Grace Produces Real Motivation

Those who live by grace know that, having already been made a perfect fit for the filling and activity of the Holy Spirit, offering themselves to Him is the primary step toward finding His grace sufficient for all of life. Those who offer themselves will find perfect love and the grace of God. Toward what end? They'll know what kind of service to render and to whom, how much money to give and where, what to say or not say, what to do or not do, what to like or not like, and more. For you and me, it's the way of life, and it keeps heaven in view.

Because many people have lost the view of heaven, they've lost the love and joy and grace and motivation that come from it. Though I believe they are secure for eternity, Christ is of no value, no current effect to them (see Galatians 5:2)—they're lacking life. *They're in neutral.* But that doesn't mean they aren't busy revving their engines and honking their horns, even urging others to do the same. It's what they know. If you and I try to get them to quit their anxious foot-stomping and horn-honking without telling them of the grace of God toward them in Christ, we'll just be encouraging them to cease hyperactivity for *no* activity. If we don't introduce them to heaven's view, they'll still be lifeless—zombies on parade.

What can you do? Keep your own fire lit and your own thirst quenched. It may sound selfish, but pretended heat and postured satisfaction are problems enough in the church without you succumbing as well.

When people attempt to light fires and create thirst in others over many years of ministry, disappointment in how people receive the truth has at times led to deep personal disillusionment. I have been led away from the very passion and delight I've found with God by putting my own attempts with *other people* first. While believing that they are His workmanship, I sometimes fall victim to thinking I might help Him out a bit. In that misguided attempt, I can get awfully cold and thirsty and have little to offer. Think of it this way: The best cup from which to drink is the full one—not the empty one.

You will be brought before many challenging and trying situations. But the greatest challenge and highest goal is to keep knowing Jesus and His view of you and everything else. On the job, in your relationships, in your hopes, in your dreams, in your failures, and in your successes (and you will find plenty of both), knowing Him as your greatest treasure will mean satisfaction for you and hope for others. You've sold off everything and bought the field, having discovered Him as your treasure. Pay attention to it, marvel at it, and the by-product will be the style of life God intends for you and for His glory. Out of love for God, you'll give the gospel and forgive those who preach a twisted version. You'll see what heaven sees, and you'll passionately desire to relieve believers of their earthborn view.

You'll be living from God's astounding opinion of you. Understanding your real identity will lead you to happily tell others about God's astounding opinion of them too. What a plan.

This is my prayer for you:

> I pray that out of his glorious riches he may strengthen
> you with power through his Spirit in your inner being, so

that Christ may dwell in your hearts through faith. And I pray that you, being rooted and established in love, may have power, together with all the saints, to grasp how wide and long and high and deep is the love of Christ, and to know this love that surpasses knowledge—that you may be filled to the measure of all the fullness of God. Now to him who is able to do immeasurably more than all we ask or imagine, according to his power that is at work within us, to him be glory in the church and in Christ Jesus throughout all generations, for ever and ever! Amen (Ephesians 3:16-21).

Questions for Discussion

1. If heaven were to confine its view only to you for a few moments, what would happen next?

2. What is heaven celebrating?

3. What happens if we delight ourselves in the Lord?

4. What was the Galatian lie, and can you see it today?

5. How does grace motivate us to do something?

6. How might living by grace look for you?

Personal Notes

Personal Notes

Personal Notes

Personal Notes

Personal Notes

Personal Notes

Personal Notes

Personal Notes

_____

_____

_____

_____

_____

_____

_____

_____

_____

_____

_____

_____

_____

_____

_____

_____

_____

_____

_____

Personal Notes

Personal Notes

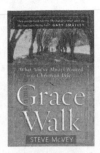

Grace Walk
What You've Always Wanted in the Christian Life
STEVE McVEY

Nothing you have ever done, nothing you could ever do, will match the incomparable joy of letting Jesus live His life through you. It is what makes the fire of passion burn so brightly in new believers. And it is what causes the light of contentment to shine in the eyes of mature believers who are growing in the grace walk. As you relax in Jesus and delight in His love and friendship, you'll find that He will do more *through you* and *in you* than you could ever do for Him or for yourself.

Lifetime Guarantee
Making Your Christian Life Work and What to Do When It Doesn't
BILL GILLHAM

You've tried fixing your marriage, your kids, and your job. Suddenly, the light dawns. It's not your problems that need fixing, it's your life! The good news is that the Christian is backed by God's lifetime guarantee.

Becoming Who God Intended
• A New Picture for Your Past • A Healthy Way of Managing Your Emotions • A Fresh Perspective on Relationships
DAVID ECKMAN

Every person's "heart life" is filled with *pictures* of reality—often false ones, says David Eckman. But as believers use the truth of their new identity in Christ to develop *biblical* pictures, they will be able to truly accept God's acceptance of them, be freed from negative emotions and habitual sins…and finally experience a life that matches what Scripture promises.

For information about Ralph Harris and LifeCourse
Ministries, please visit www.LifeCourse.org.

To book Ralph Harris for speaking engagements,
please contact him at Ralph@LifeCourse.org.

To catch up with Ralph right now…
www.Facebook.com
www.LifeCourseMinistries.blogspot.com